A Fulhamish Tale

A Fulhamish Tale

David Hamilton

ASHWATER
PRESS

Designed and published by
Ashwater Press
68 Tranmere Road, Whitton, Twickenham, Middlesex, TW2 7JB

www.ashwaterpress.co.uk

Printed by Ian Allan Printing, Hersham, Surrey

ISBN 978-0-9562561-6-4

Contents

Craven Cottage

I first saw Fulham play as a schoolboy. Johnny Haynes, Tosh Chamberlain and Jimmy Hill – much later to become my colleague and friend – were in the side. I remember Jimmy covering every inch of the pitch. Nowadays he would be called a box-to-box player but it didn't prevent him getting dog's abuse from Johnny for the odd stray pass.

Thirty years later I found myself reporting on the team which included George Best and Bobby Moore.

I always loved going to The Cottage and still do now just for pleasure – such a delightful and friendly place to watch the game with civilised fans whose humour and sense of irony is well honed. A Saturday afternoon walking along by the Thames with the prospect of a Premier League game to look forward to makes everything seem alright with the world.

Des Lynam OBE

I love going to Fulham because it has one of the best commentary positions in the Premier League, directly above the half-way line.

The other reason is I always find a warm, friendly atmosphere wherever I go in the stadium – a delightful and civilised place to watch football.

John Motson OBE

Acknowledgements

My thanks to Ken Coton for his photographic pearls, his Ashwater thoroughness and infinite patience. Also thanks to Alan Mullery, Four Four Two, David Lloyd and TOOFIF, Liverpool FC, Dorothy Ravenswood, Jason Bowyer, Robert Fennell, Martin Plumb, Fulham FC, Alan Williams, Peter Thomson, David Shrimpton, Michael Hoodless, Ian Allan Printing and all who have helped during the writing and production of this book.

Foreword

from Alan Mullery MBE

I can't believe it's fifty years since I first met David Hamilton. He was a budding broadcaster and I was a young footballer breaking into Fulham's first team.

I immediately liked him because it rapidly became clear that his passion for football equalled his passion for music and such was his love for Fulham that if he bled, it would surely come out black and white. Little did I know in those early days that both our careers would take off into orbit. David became a national name on Radio 1, Radio 2 and *Top of the Pops* and I was lucky enough to play for two major London clubs and to captain teams that won the FA Cup, the League Cup and the UEFA Cup and also to captain the England team, for whom I played 35 times.

Throughout this time we have been firm friends, enjoying many dinners together, lots of them with our mutual friend Ray Jenkins. One thing these occasions have in common – there has always been lots of laughter around the table. I even went to see David in pantomime – Oh, yes I did! – when he took the mickey out of me from the stage. When he was younger he was a bit 'wild', but I'm happy to say he has calmed down a bit!

As you will read in this book, I gave David what he describes as 'one of the biggest thrills of my life' when I asked him to play in a very special football match. As it happens, David wasn't a bad player, though I have to say his football career hasn't equalled my broadcasting career! I do believe he has learned a lot about the game from working with the likes of George Cohen and myself.

There's nobody better equipped to write a book about Fulham. He's been there, in front of and behind the scenes, for a lifetime during which he has seen the club almost go out of business and then climb from Division Three to the cream of the Premier League with an FA Cup final and a EUFA final thrown in.

Bearing in mind what he has done for the club down the years, it's true to say that David is indeed a Fulham legend.

Going to the match – 2011 style. Through Bishops Park to Craven Cottage.

FULHAMISH *full'əm'ish n (origin early 20th century)* quirky, eccentric, capricious, as in the football club on the banks of the River Thames

THIS IS a story about London's oldest football league club and of a boy who has followed it throughout his life – from standing behind the goal as a nine-year-old to joining the board of directors, playing in testimonial matches with international soccer stars and eventually becoming the club's matchday MC during the glory years that included three promotions, a European final and the club's longest ever run in England's top division.

But why 'Fulhamish'? Well, what club could take more matches than any other to get to a Wembley cup final, winning them all away from home, playing scintillating football, only to freeze on the big day?

And then years later beat some of the world's greatest clubs on the way to a European final only to lose to a goal at the end of extra time?

Which club could clinch promotion, only to lose the final match of the season at home to the team who would then beat them to the championship?

Or win 10–1 against a team who two days later would beat them 4–2*?

Which Premier League club could have what looks like a cricket pavilion in one corner and the statue of a pop star in another?

Or have two of its players tackle each other to get the ball forgetting they were on the same team?

Which club has a chairman who does a lap of honour before every game?

This is about a club that was once on its knees, in grave danger of dropping out of the Football League and losing its ancestral home – and of its incredible resurrection, told by a fan who was there in the good years and the bad.

---

* *Ipswich, 1963*

To the Black and White Army.

And to Mohamed Al Fayed, who made the Fulham dream come true.

Chapter 1

A Lucky Escape

This Fulhamish tale begins at Ranelagh Gardens Mansions, SW6, a block of flats next to Putney Bridge tube station that millions of football supporters have walked past on their way to the game. In 1949 my mother moved into number 25, a ground floor flat there, with the Liverpudlian army officer she had met during the war. My father, a journalist, was a conscripted corporal fighting with the infantry in Italy where he was shot and finished up in hospital, but Jack was a regular soldier who never left his home country or heard a shot fired in anger. Such are the ironies of war. My father's reward was to come home and discover his wife was in love with another man.

The flat itself wasn't up to much. So that there could be a second bedroom for me, the bath was in the kitchen underneath the table top. To take a bath we had first to remove the table top and its contents. Consequently, none of us bathed as often as we should. The flat was damp – in my bedroom I could see damp patches on the wall – and it came with hot and cold running mice, which joined us from the nearby riverbank. The only good thing about it was that it was incredibly handy for both the tube station and the local football ground.

A left turn out of the flats past Barnett, the Jewish tailor, a greengrocer and the station newsagent and you were on the District Line into town. A right turn took you through Bishops Park, along the River Thames, to Craven Cottage, home of Fulham Football Club. On match days there was a buzz that went right through the area. It seemed to start in Putney High Street, sweep over the bridge and head into the park. It also came from the tube station, right past our ground floor flat. Living in Ranelagh Gardens Mansions, I could hear the urgent patter of feet and the hubbub of chatter as people passed the window. Some stopped for a drink at the Eight Bells, the pub built into our block of flats. There was little vandalism. Sometimes people passing

BEFORE AND AFTER THE MATCH

THE **EIGHT BELLS**

PUTNEY BRIDGE
(UNDERGROUND STATION)]

From the Fulham programme in the 1950s.

would tap on the window and occasionally someone returning in the dark to the station would pee up against the wall.

The surrounding area was very different then. Where the budget hotel now stands in front of the Eight Bells was a motor mart. The hideous Sixties building across the road from it took the place of an old theatre, the Fulham Empire, and on the other side the fashionable flats on the river were then spooky, disused wharves. The Fulham matchday experience began at the arch under Putney Bridge where you could buy rosettes of both the home and away teams, as well as rattles and programmes. Because people had been known to print 'rogue' programmes, supporters were urged to buy the 'official matchday programme'. No-one in the area could be in any doubt there was a match on that day. Fulham had won promotion in 1949 and were playing in the First Division, the top league in the country. When Chelsea or Arsenal came to visit, crowds

A street photographer took this shot of my father and me on the way to my first football match at Chelsea. Lots of them operated near football grounds. You'd give them your address and the money, and they'd send you the picture. Some unscrupulous ones had no film in their camera. On this occasion we were lucky.

were around the 45,000 mark, nearly twice what they are today.

My father also lived near a football ground, though one far less exciting. His council flat in Moffat Court, Gap Road, led down to Plough Lane, home of Wimbledon FC, then playing in the Isthmian League. Dad was a Chelsea supporter and took me to see my first football match at Stamford Bridge. I didn't like the ground much. There was a greyhound track around the pitch and, as a nine-year-old boy, I was too far away from the action. I remember they had a winger called 'Rabbit' Parsons and I wondered if he got his nickname because he shot up and down the wing a bit like the racing hare.

My parents' divorce was so acrimonious that they never spoke to each other again and so there were never any calls between RENown 2275 and LIBerty 5403. This did lead to some misunderstandings. One year they both asked me what I would like for Christmas. I mentioned that what I really wanted was a drop handlebar racing bike, while knowing that since neither of them had much money, it was unlikely that I would get one. On Christmas Day

View of the riverside terracing in the mid-Sixties, complete with state-of-the-art electronic scoreboard and TV camera gantry atop a tea bar – plus flags of all Division One clubs.

I woke to find a shiny red bike in the passage at Ranelagh Gardens. After lunch I cycled from Fulham to Wimbledon to see my father and his second wife, Delia. When they opened the door, their faces dropped. There in the hallway was another drop handlebar bike. Two bikes – fine for me, not so good for them.

Jack was a Liverpool supporter and when his team came to town in October 1949, he took me to my first match at Craven Cottage. We stood on the open terraces on the river side among a crowd of 42,000. Opposite on the roof of the Stevenage Road Stand was a huge sign proclaiming 'Fulham Football and Athletic Co Ltd'. I never knew why there was a reference to athletics because none seemed to take place there, although there was a running track around the pitch. The ground, I remember, was very cold. With no stand on the river side, the wind whipped in off the Thames blowing through the flags of the Division One clubs. A hot cup of Bovril at half-time warmed us up. They say you always remember your first match and you may even remember your first team. Mine at Fulham was: Hugh Kelly, Harry Freeman, Joe Bacuzzi, Len Quested, Jim Taylor, Pat Beasley, Arthur Stevens, Bob Thomas, Arthur Rowley, Bedford Jezzard and Sid Thomas. Fulham lost 1–nil, but at least Jack was happy. After that first game we went to Fulham quite a lot. When Jack didn't take me, I started to go on my own and stood near the railings behind the goal at the Putney end, as close to the action as I could get. By now I had decided that Fulham, not Chelsea, would be my team. A lucky escape.

On the day of the Varsity Boat Race, the crowd would turn round and watch the Oxford and Cambridge crews row past. It was a really odd experience to see a crowd at a football match turn away from the action on the pitch. Maybe the Boat Race was more exciting.

After the match we would buy fish and chips from the chip shop on Fulham High Street. It would be wrapped up in newspaper and soaked in vinegar. By six o'clock we'd pick up the Pink 'un, the evening newspaper that contained the classified football results, up-to-date league tables and a report on at least the first half of that afternoon's matches. Even as a young boy, it never ceased to amaze me that all this could be written, edited, printed and then delivered to the streets of a London suburb in such a short time.

Though the Fulham Empire had closed, there was another theatre not far away – the Granville, close to Walham Green tube station, later renamed Fulham Broadway. The Granville staged non-stop variety and one evening my mother, Jack and I went along to see the show. One of the acts was called 'Annette's Lovely Nudes', young ladies who appeared in tableaux but by law were not allowed to move. I had already invested a shilling in the opera glasses on the back of the seat in front of me and, never having seen a naked woman, it occurred to me that these could come in handy for what might be a very enlightening experience. I didn't realise at the time that the ladies were wearing sticking plaster over their private parts and, as a curious thirteen-year-old, I was disappointed to find them as unexciting as the mannequins waiting to be draped in the windows of the shops in Putney High Street. A ventriloquist followed the nude ladies on the continuous bill and Jack and I managed to persuade my mother that he was so good that we should stay on to see his act again. As the girls reappeared, out came the opera glasses but sadly the second house was no more revealing. Fortunately, future sightings of the opposite sex proved to be more entertaining.

There was something very showbizzy about Fulham FC in the Fifties, which was not surprising with Tommy Trinder, the Cockney comedian, as the chairman, and bandleader 'Chappie' D'Amato on the board. Honor Blackman and Harry Fowler were regulars in the Stevenage Road Stand. Harry and Kenny 'Kipper' Lynch were banned by ITV when they appeared on the TV pop show *Ready Steady Go* wielding the placard 'Alcock and Brown'. "He's Brown," said Kenny, pointing at Harry. Today it would be regarded as harmless fun, tame compared with what passes as comedy on a Saturday night, but in those days the bosses were not amused. Fulham were the butt of many of Tommy Trinder's jokes and, as he admitted, when they did well they ruined his act. One Trinder gem I recall: "My wife's got a Fulham bra – plenty of support but no cups."

Bobby Robson's sunny smile.   *Johnny Haynes runs out.*

Tommy Trinder ran into trouble with the Football Association when he gave winger Arthur Stevens an overcoat. He promised it to Arthur if he scored 15 league goals in a season, an incredible tally for a winger. When Arthur did and Tommy gave him the present, the FA accused the Fulham chairman of making an illegal payment. Arthur was part of an exciting forward line that Fulham had in the Fifties. The inside trio was dazzling: Bobby Robson, whom Fulham signed despite stiff competition from the teams in his native north east, Bedford Jezzard, a high scoring centre-forward capped by England, whose career ended prematurely when he broke a leg on a tour of South Africa

at the age of 29, and the Brylcreem boy, Johnny Haynes, whose face, like Denis Compton's, adorned railway stations around the country. Haynes played 56 times for England, 22 as captain, and was reckoned to be the finest passer of a ball in living memory. George Cohen describes him as having 'incredible vision', by which I guess he means that he had eyes in the back of his head and always knew where his team-mates were. All this made him the first footballer to earn £100 a week, and that was thanks to the efforts of his Fulham colleague Jimmy Hill who, as chairman

The Brylcreem boy.

Ian Black; right: Trevor Chamberlain celebrates a match-winning goal by Johnny Haynes at West Ham in the FA Cup in 1958.

of the PFA, brought about the abolition of the maximum wage in 1961. That was one of the many gifts Jimmy gave to football along with the action replay on *Match Of The Day* and three points, instead of two, for a win.

If Johnny Haynes was a highly gifted player, he was also highly demanding of and frustrated by his colleagues. Much of his annoyance was taken out on the man who encouraged him to come to Fulham in the first place and became his room-mate on away games – the mercurial Trevor 'Tosh' Chamberlain, who occupied the left wing position alongside Johnny. Tosh had a kick like a mule and probably the hardest shot of anyone in the game. The only problem was that when he struck the ball it would either rip out the back of the net or wind up in the river. The statue of Johnny Haynes outside the ground today shows the maestro hands on hips, in typical matchday pose. If it could speak, it would say, "Call that a bloody pass, Tosh?" Incidentally, Fulham folklore has it that Tosh once took part in a pre-match warm-up with a cigarette cupped between his fingers, a story he has never denied. The finest tribute to the man is that when a book came out entitled *Football's Greatest Characters* an entire chapter was devoted to Tosh Chamberlain.

There are lots of players I remember from my teenage years of watching on the terraces. In goal was the stylish Scottish keeper, Ian Black. In one game, back in those days before substitutes were allowed, he returned to the pitch from injury with his arm in a sling and, playing as a forward, scored a goal

Archie Macaulay, Reg Lowe, a very young Johnny Haynes and Eddie Lowe training at the Cottage.

with his head. For thirteen seasons there was the familiar bald head of Eddie Lowe who joined the club from Aston Villa with his brother, Reg. Reg was a decent player too, and often the brothers played alongside each other but Reg's career, like Beddy Jezzard's, was ended early when he broke a leg.

Often players moved down the road to us from Chelsea, as was the case with Wally Hinshelwood and Jimmy Bowie, though previously Hinshelwood had made the move from Craven Cottage to Stamford Bridge. Generally, their players came to us, rather than the other way round. Strange that, isn't it?

Many colourful characters came to Fulham during the Fifties. Much excitement was caused by the arrival of the former Manchester United winger Charlie Mitten, although most of the publicity surrounded his six-month suspension for playing in Bogota. A crowd of 45,000 turned up for his first match, at home to Chelsea, in January 1952, and in the next match he scored two goals in Fulham's 6–nil trouncing of Middlesbrough.

These were some of the players I watched in my youth. The Fulham players were referred to in the programme, unbelievably, as wearing 'white shirts and

That's me on the right with my friend Michael Skinner outside Ranelagh Gardens Mansions before a kick-about in Bishops Park.

black knickers'. The first time I saw a player not in white shirt and black knickers came when I was kicking a ball around in Bishops Park with my pal Michael Skinner, who lived in the flat above mine in Ranelagh Gardens Mansions. Along the footpath came a smart figure in a blazer and flannels. "Look," I said to Michael. "It's Bobby Robson." We stood in awe as he passed by, far too shy to ask for his autograph. Shame, because it could have been worth a few bob in time to come.

In the Fifties every club had its star player. Blackpool had Stanley Matthews, Preston Tom Finney, Bolton Nat Lofthouse, Wolves Billy Wright and Charlton had Sam Bartram. I first saw Bartram play at Fulham and with his bright red hair and green jersey he stood out from the other players on the pitch. He was also a showman and went to places where goalkeepers are not supposed to go. He'd run out of the penalty area, take off his cap and head the ball away or he'd dribble it up to the half-way line. He gave a superhuman performance at Fulham that day and I have to confess that although Fulham have always been my team, Sam Bartram was my favourite player until he retired in 1956 at the age of 42.

Not surprisingly with Sam as my inspiration, I started out as a goalkeeper in the under 11 team when I was a boarder at Kingswood House School in Epsom but I got the message when an entry in the school magazine said: 'David

Pilditch [David Hamilton Pilditch was my full name until I later changed it] was the most promising member of the under 11s. With a few more inches, he could be a useful player.' The story of my life. I took the hint and realised that I might be better off playing out on the wing.

After leaving Kingswood House I got a place at Glastonbury Road Grammar School on the St Helier estate in Surrey. The English master, Mr

Me (at left in front row) with the all-conquering Glastonbury Road football team.

Hawkins, also ran the school football team and he was very keen that we should do well. We didn't let him down and won the St. Helier District League every season. We were nigh on unbeatable and David Gardner, who followed on a couple of years later and went on to become a Fulham director, tells me that he and his peers kept the winning run going. The success of the school team and some outings for the district XI led me to believe that maybe I could look forward to a career in football and I applied for a trial for Wimbledon. I didn't get taken on and I think I knew that although I had some good touches, I didn't have the killer instinct, the toughness you need to play at the very top.

If I wasn't going to earn a living playing the game, perhaps the next best thing was to write about it.

February 26, 1955

Soccer Star, February 26, 1955

THE NATIONAL SOCCER WEEKLY

Soccer STAR

6D

David Pilditch surveys
LONDON

"THIS is our best season for a long while," is what London fans are saying just now. They certainly have no cause to complain about the soccer their clubs are serving up every week.

Look at the Third Division (South). Here the "Cinderella" club, Leyton Orient, are running away with promotion. Manager Alec Stock has certainly moulded together a first-class combination.

And not far behind the "O's" are Charlie Hewitt's Millwall who, year in, year out, are up with the Third South leaders. After an indefinite start to the season, the "Lions" are producing some rip-roaring soccer. Seems they're too late for promotion, but watch them next season!

Queen's Park Rangers, too, are an enterprising outfit, among the best in the division. A pity they're rather erratic. On too many occasions this season they have been held to a draw when wins would have been very helpful to them.

In his first full playing season at Griffin Park, manager Bill Dodgin has made it evident that he fully intends to bring Second Division soccer back to Brentford. Asked what chance there was of a promotion-seeking Brentford next season, Mr. Dodgin replied, "The impossible we do at once miracles take a little longer!" The "Bees" certainly have youth on their side.

Another manager who is getting straight down to business is Cyril Spiers of Crystal Palace. Mr. Spiers has decided to concentrate on youth and the future is bright for the Palace.

London's two Second Division sides, Fulham and West Ham, are both enterprising teams, strong in attack. Fulham's defence still needs tightening and I can only suggest that the club dips into its finances and buys a class full-back. A defensive wing-half is also on order at Craven Cottage.

West Ham, with their abundance of youth, are still very much in the promotion hunt. Another experienced forward like Les Bennett might help. Like Fulham, the Hammers have conceded rather too many goals.

(Continued on page 13)

Read about . . .
Ye Olde
Football

on pages 8 & 9

JIMMY SCOULAR

There were a lot of heavy hearts at Portsmouth when Jimmy Scoular left to join Newcastle, for he was one of the club's most popular players. Equally well liked at Newcastle is skipper Jimmy (our exclusive photo shows him leading out his team at Chelsea recently). Now turn to page five for the photo of Jimmy's team.

I make the front page of Soccer Star, aged 16.

Chapter 2

Soccer Star

There were two super football magazines in the Fifties, both fronted by former players – *Charles Buchan's Football Monthly* and Raich Carter's weekly *Soccer Star*. Every Thursday a copy of *Soccer Star* would drop on the mat at 25 Ranelagh Gardens Mansions, delivered by the newsagent in Putney Bridge station. I would devour it from cover to cover. In the summer of 1954, with all the wisdom of a fifteen-year-old schoolboy, I reckoned that in the long close season that football then had, they might be short of material so I sent them an article which, to my surprise and delight, they printed. Beneath it the by-line said 'David Pilditch, who submitted this article, is one of our old and regular readers.'

Well, certainly regular! Armed with this success, I wrote to the editor and asked if he would be interested in my writing a weekly column. Again, to my great surprise, he answered yes and said that they would pay me two guineas (two pounds and two shillings – £2.10) per article. Thus every week I set off to different grounds in London to watch the games and come back with my stories. I never thought to get a press pass but paid at the turnstile like everyone else and then took up my favourite place behind the goal. One week I'd be at Fulham, the next at Chelsea, then Charlton and so on. It gave me plenty of opportunities to write about my favourite club.

In January 1955, I wrote a Soccertale about Jimmy Hill which included this paragraph: 'Fulham's supporters have come to respect his soccer ability. This energetic wing-half with the prominent chin and long legs has earned many admirers with his non-stop 90-minute play. And his loyalty to the club, both on and off the field, have won him the captaincy of the Fulham side, in which capacity he is an inspiration and driving force behind his colleagues.'

In April 1955, I was happy to report in *Soccer Star*:

'Fulham beat West Ham United in the final of the London Five-A-Side Football Championship at Harringay. Fulham played extremely skilful soccer.

'Five-a-side football is adopted by many clubs as a training device. The ball must be kept below head height, and is hardly ever dead. There are no

Fulham 5-a-side champions. Bobby Robson, Jimmy Hill, Johnny Haynes, Ian Black and Eddie Lowe.

throw-ins, goal kicks, etc, and the duration of play is eight minutes each way. Fulham's team – Ian Black, Eddie Lowe, Jimmy Hill, Johnny Haynes and Bobby Robson – found their men well, kept the ball on the ground and generally impressed as experienced in the game.

'In the semi-final Fulham beat the holders, Charlton, 5–1. Bobby Robson notched a hat-trick. In the final Fulham scored an easy victory over West Ham.

'Ten thousand spectators spent a very enjoyable evening and all the teams had large followings. The teams competing were London First and Second Division clubs.'

It was not really surprising that Fulham won with a line-up like that, and goalkeeper Ian Black was the subject of another Soccertale I wrote in *Soccer Star* in June 1955.

By the time I left school I had been writing my column for 15 months and at two guineas a week I was a well-off teenager. Time to get a job, and where better or more obvious than at *Soccer Star* so I made an appointment to see the editor at his office in Cheapside. When I got there, I don't know who was more surprised, him or me. I was amazed to find that my favourite magazine could emerge from such untidy offices with articles and photographs strewn all over the floor and he was amazed to find that his columnist was a schoolboy who'd just turned 17! "From the way you wrote, we thought you were about forty," he said.

There followed a tough lesson early in life. Not only did I not get a staff job, but they swiftly dropped my column. Embarrassed that people might find out that one of their star columnists was a schoolboy? That's the only reason I can think of. It taught me that you don't always get the result you expect or think you deserve. Being a Fulham supporter, I should have known that.

From the picture album

Pete Murray, my broadcasting mentor, is a welcome guest at Craven Cottage.

Chapter 3

It's Only Rock 'n' Roll

As a teenager growing up in the Fifties, I had two great passions. One was football. The other was rock 'n' roll. We were the first generation growing up after the war and we rejected our parents' music. Now we had music of our own. The problem was that the BBC ignored it and refused to play it. The only way to hear rock 'n' roll was to listen at night to Radio Luxembourg. With its signal fading in and out, it wasn't ideal but the music was great and the star DJ was definitely Pete Murray. He was funny and his shows were fun. One day I saw a photo of him in a magazine called *Fab 208* (the Luxembourg wavelength). It showed him horse-riding in the Grand Duchy of Luxembourg. What a glamorous job, I thought, horse-riding and answering his fan mail by day and playing records at night, just the kind of job I'd like. But, hang on, there were only four disc-jockeys from the UK, and they were all in Luxembourg.

If I wasn't going to be a professional footballer, if I wasn't going to write for *Soccer Star* and if I wasn't going to be Pete Murray Mark 2, I must, as my father reminded me, get a job of some kind. Independent Television was a new industry and when I joined it I started right at the bottom – as a post boy in the mail room of ATV, one of the newly opened commercial stations, based in Kingsway. I had to collect and deliver the mail of the great and good like Lew Grade and Val Parnell. I didn't see much of the great men, but more of their secretaries who would ask me to nip out to the shops and buy them some cigarettes.

Merciful release came after six months when I got chatting to Harold Jamieson, head of ATV's script department. I told him about the articles I'd written for *Soccer Star* and, as luck would have it, that week I had an article published in *TV Times* which Jamieson had seen. More luck was coming my way. One of his writers, Tessa Diamond, had come up with the idea of the first TV soap drama set in a hospital, *Emergency Ward 10*, and was concentrating on writing the scripts for that. Jamieson needed someone to replace her and offered me a job as a staff scriptwriter for ATV. At the age of 18 I wrote my first programme script. On a Sunday night my mother and some friends and I sat

Germany calling! There's no truth in the rumour that I started broadcasting under the name of Lord Haw-Haw.

Aged 19 in Germany I meet a pop star for the first time, the Marilyn Monroe-esque Marion Ryan. The next visitor to Cologne was Cliff Richard, promoting his record Livin' Doll.

round the black-and-white TV set at Ranelagh Gardens Mansions and watched my first TV credit come up at the end of *Portrait Of A Star*: 'Script by David Pilditch.'

Everything was going well with my new job when one day a buff envelope dropped on the mat at RGM bearing news that would take me away from my job at ATV, from my first girlfriend and from watching Fulham. I'd been called up for National Service which meant two years in the forces, in which I had absolutely no interest. For a start, I hated guns and felt the man who invented them should have been shot. But there was no choice. I was drafted into the RAF, given a number and paid a pittance. After square-bashing and training as a wireless operator at camps in the UK, I was miraculously posted to Cologne in Germany, home of the British Forces Network radio and also the German link on the big record show of the time, *Two Way Family Favourites*, the programme that was an institution on Sunday lunchtimes and was once described as the

Roy Bentley on his debut at Craven Cottage.

only radio show that had its own smell – roast beef and Yorkshire pudding.

Once in Cologne I offered my services to the station manager, telling him that my actual profession was scriptwriter. He told me he needed someone to read the football results and, as a fan of *Sports Report*, I told him that was right up my street. Listening to that programme, I knew it was all about the right inflections: "Chelsea One, Fulham TWO". (Dream on.)

Reading the results for the rest of that 1958–59 season turned out to be a pleasure. Fulham hardly lost another game. They rounded off the season beating Rotherham 4–nil. Johnny Haynes scored a hat-trick and Fulham were promoted. Gradually, the radio station gave me more programmes and ultimately let me have my own rock 'n' roll show on Sunday afternoons. It was a very exciting time in Germany because Elvis Presley was there at the same time with the US Army, and on my show I played Elvis's records along with the likes of Little Richard and Jerry Lee Lewis. Until then all the music on the

Soon after leaving Fulham, Alan Mullery lines up as Spurs captain and comes up against Johnny Haynes.

station had been jazz or standards so finally the troops had their own music, and they loved it. It was also in Germany that I acquired a new name. The station manager suggested that Pilditch might be a difficult name for people to grasp over the radio and it was agreed that I would adopt my mother's maiden name and become David Hamilton.

Eventually, my two years' service was up and I returned to the UK in time for the start of a new decade which would be known as the Swinging Sixties. When I arrived home one of my first calls had to be to Craven Cottage. The old place looked the same but there were many new faces. Roy Bentley, who I remembered as a centre-forward at Chelsea – 'bustling' is the word they used in those days – had been converted to a 'stopper' centre-half, a real hard man.

To David
Best Wishes
J. ......

Fulham supporter Colin Davis gave me this photograph. One of his employees, Jimmy Langley's daughter-in-law Jill, got Jimmy to sign this a week before he died in 2007. It was the last of many autographs that Jimmy signed. In the picture Jimmy is third right in the back row. Other players in the back row are (from left) George Cohen, Alan Mullery, Tony Macedo, Eddie Lowe and Derek Lampe. Seated are Johnny Key, Brian O'Connell, Johnny Haynes, John Doherty and Trevor Watson.

George Cohen was a raiding right back. At left back with his crew-cut and bandy legs was Jim Langley, an early exponent of the bicycle kick. He played against Stanley Matthews in the legend's last league match at the age of 50. George and Jim were as fine a pair of full-backs as you'd see anywhere in the first division. In goal was the acrobatic Tony Macedo, who would go on to play 400 games for the club. On the right wing was Graham Leggat, a Scottish international. He was fast, brave, direct and scored a lot of goals – 134 in 277 appearances. Wearing the number 4 shirt was Alan Mullery, a strong, lion-hearted player who would be sold to Spurs four years later. Fulham, as usual, needed the money. Mullery was happy at Craven Cottage, but the board decided to sell him. It turned out to be a good move for Alan, who went on to become an England captain, playing for his country 35 times.

Other things had changed at home, too. Jack, my mother's boyfriend, died at the age of 50 and my mother had taken a job as a sales girl, eventually becoming manageress at Richard Shops in Putney High Street. I'd only been home for ten months when a job came up that would take me out of London for several years. In fact, I had a year as an announcer and programme presenter for Tyne Tees Television in Newcastle followed by seven years doing the same for ABC Television in Manchester, so visits to my favourite football club were few and far between.

Late in 1968 I moved back to London as announcer and programme presenter for Thames TV at the Kingsway studios where I'd started as a scriptwriter. Sadly, my mother died in 1970, aged just 58, and Roz, my girlfriend at the time, and I took over the tenancy at Ranelagh Gardens Mansions. Not much had changed there; even the hot and cold running mice were still around and the bath was still in the kitchen. But we loved sunny days sitting by the river in Bishops Park, watching the world go by, and in no time she was coming with me to matches at Fulham. I'd had my two years away in the RAF and the best part of the Sixties up north. Now I was back in London and this would be my longest uninterrupted run of watching the Whites, which would continue for more than four decades.

Chapter 4

Dirty Fulham

"Dirty Fulham!" she shouted, leaping out of her seat incensed by a foul committed by a Doncaster player.

"Sit down," I pleaded. It was halfway through the second half and she thought Doncaster were playing in black and white. Johnny Haynes had gone by now, but there was exciting talent on view. It wasn't a great team, though it had some good individuals, but it was too good for the third division. Malcolm Webster was probably Fulham's fattest goalkeeper until Big Jim Stannard came along. Freddie Callaghan was a warhorse of a player, nicknamed 'The Tank', at left back. Stan Brown, a good little worker, covered every blade of grass on the pitch. Reg Matthewson was a tall, commanding centre-half. Out on the right wing was Jimmy Conway with his unusual style, crouched over the ball as though it was tied to his laces with a piece of string. Jimmy went on to become one of the club's most popular and talented players in a career dogged by injuries. On the left was Les Barrett, who personified the wing man – and what a devastating effect he could have on a game. With the speed of a greyhound, he was down the line, leaving the full-back for dead, right down to the goal-line getting in behind the defence and then delivering a perfectly placed cross to the big man in the middle. Once in a match against Sunderland I saw him turn their full-back, big Dick Malone – no slouch, by the way – inside out. He beat him inside, then outside and nutmegged him for good measure. By the end of the match I could swear Dick was almost in tears. Manchester United and Tottenham both wanted to sign Les, but he only wanted to play for Fulham. I watched Les on Saturday afternoons, and then on Sundays tried to copy what he did when I played in charity matches. Unfortunately, it didn't quite work out like that.

There was a bit of a hiccup to Fulham's season with three successive defeats as we went into December 1970, and then there was the perfect Christmas. On Christmas Eve I went to a party at the Esher home of songwriter Barry Mason, the man who wrote *Delilah*, which became a huge football anthem. It snowed that night and when we left at 2 o'clock on Christmas

Stan Brown

Jimmy Conway

Les Barrett

Fred Callaghan

The team celebrates promotion on the Cottage balcony, but manager Bill Dodgin doesn't join in, disappointed at not having won the championship.

morning the countryside was covered in snow. It was the perfect white Christmas, and the Whites' Christmas was perfect, too, with a win on the 28th. Seven thousand of us hardy souls shivered as Fulham on almost unplayable conditions beat Gillingham 1–nil with one of 25 goals to come from Vic Halom.

The stylish Steve Earle was bagging plenty of goals, too. We'd lost only one game at home, and that to Aston Villa, amazingly then only in the third division. We'd spent the first half of the season in the top four and as we went into 1971 we became increasingly confident of promotion. We clinched it in April with wins at Doncaster and Bradford City.

Nearly 26,000 turned up for the last match against Preston North End, a remarkable crowd for a Division Three team. All we needed was a draw to go up as champions. But Preston needed a win to clinch promotion. They beat us 1–nil and there was a sickening scene as their manager, Alan Ball senior, father of the England International, rushed on to the pitch and kissed the turf. At that moment I hated him. Preston had ruined our day of celebration, but all that really mattered was that we were out of that damned third division. After my time away, I'd really caught that Fulham bug again. The best was yet to come – and the worst, too.

A Fulhamish end to the season, as a fan is pictured ready to celebrate a championship, but has to settle for second place. Cheer up! At least we gained promotion!

From the picture album

At Roy Bentley's 80th birthday party I give him a photo of himself with one of the world's most beautiful women, Ava Gardner. No wonder he's smiling.

Chapter 5

Playing for Kicks

Winning promotion but missing out on being champions on their home turf was something that, as I was to discover over and over again, could only be described as 'Fulhamish'. Nonetheless, Fulham were back in Division Two and there they would stay for a long time. As well as watching the lads on Saturdays, I spent most Sundays playing football for the Showbiz XI which took part in charity matches, often on league grounds and against ex-pros. The team had been formed in the late Fifties and, long before I played, star players had been personalities like David Frost, Sean Connery, Des O'Connor and Jimmy Tarbuck. Tarby once joked on television, "Seeing Des O'Connor in the shower after a Showbiz XI game reminded me to buy some button mushrooms on the way home."

Showbiz XI matches were fun days out for the singers, actors and comedians who made up the team. The games kept us fit but there was always plenty of laughter and practical jokes. Once in the restaurant car of a train heading for a game in the west country Ray Davies of The Kinks and Larry Taylor, who did many of the stunts on the James Bond films, were sitting opposite a couple of elderly ladies. Soon after the journey started they put their hands on the table and the two ladies noticed they were handcuffed to each other. From their conversation it soon emerged that Ray was an escaped convict and Larry was the warder taking him back to gaol in Exeter. As the journey wore on Ray came up with the suggestion that at some point Larry might 'spring' him, allowing him to get free, and that there might be a lot of money in it for him. After several protestations of "More than my job's worth," the amount of money became so high that Larry was being severely tempted. "How would it be done?" he enquired.

"A small scuffle on the train. I get the key out of your pocket. You get a black eye and the money."

The rest of the team, at neighbouring tables, were in on the scam and doing their utmost to suppress laughter. The old ladies were speechless, hanging on to every word, though they probably had plenty to say to each other

On a cold day in Manchester, Kenny Lynch and I get warming hugs from Coronation Street stars Bernard Youens and Peter Adamson.

after we left the train. At least we ensured that they didn't have a dull journey.

Tony Williams was the commentator of the Showbiz XI and he did lots of gags about us on the microphone: "David Hamilton joined us on a free transfer from Subbuteo"; "Jess Conrad, the goalkeeper, is known as Cinderella – he's always late for the ball"; "Robert Powell played Jesus of Nazareth – that's why he's no good on crosses"; "We've just signed Dale Winton – to stiffen up the back four." But Tony did come unstuck when introducing a former heavyweight boxing champion at a match in Lancashire. Since the champ is still around and might come and find me, we will refer to him here as 'Mr Big'.

"At number 10 for the Showbiz XI is Mr Big," said Tony. "And if he says it's Tuesday, it's Tuesday." Mr Big strolled over to the grandstand, looked up at the commentary position and shouted, "It's f------ Sunday." "I know," said Tony, with his hand covering the microphone. "What I'm saying is, if you say it's Tuesday, it's Tuesday." "You tell 'em I know it's f------ Sunday," came the reply. Tony opened the microphone and said in a very serious voice, "Mr Big has asked me to tell you he does know it's Sunday."

On another day we were playing at Walthamstow Avenue, then a leading amateur ground. The mayor of Walthamstow was due to be presented to the players before kick-off but a previous event overran and he didn't arrive until half-time. At the end of the first half, two of the team had made acquaintance with a couple of local ladies and stayed back in the dressing room at the end of the interval to get to know them a little better. As the rest of us ran out for the second half, the mayor and mayoress strode out on to the pitch and shook hands with the players. The mayor, being a very observant man, noticed we only had nine players.

"Is this the Showbiz XI?" he asked. "Indeed it is," I said.

"Then why are there only nine men?"

I explained that two of our players were injured and receiving treatment but that they would be out soon. "Then I must meet these wounded heroes," he proclaimed.

"Ah no, you don't want to do that," I said, taking him by the arm. "We have nice seats arranged for you in the stand." "Not a bit of it," he said, as he turned on his heel and headed off in the direction of the dressing room, followed by the mayoress in full regalia and a photographer from the local newspaper. He threw open the door to be greeted by the sight of the two wounded heroes being resuscitated in a fashion not generally available on the NHS.

From the picture album

How tickled I am to work with Ken Dodd and get a nickname.

Chapter 6

A Ray of Sunshine

In 1971 I was doing a tour of appearances in Top Rank bingo halls. (I know, I get all the best jobs.) One man who made a great impression on me was the manager of the hall in East Ham. He was a livewire character called Ray Jenkins. Apart from his outgoing personality and sense of humour, I discovered that he was a Fulham supporter and from then on we would regularly meet up and sit together in the Stevenage Road Stand. Ray was so fanatical about Fulham and not missing a match that he and his wife Gwen once dashed away from a wedding to be in the ground in time for kick-off.

Ray is a big man with a big voice and there were times he used it to good effect. He came along to watch me play in a charity match at Croydon. As usual, I was out on the right wing and playing inside me was Bill Oddie. Bill wasn't a bad player – he just didn't like to get rid of the ball. He'd dribble past one player, dribble past a second but by the time he got to the third, he'd usually lose it. I, meanwhile, was running into space and getting more and more frustrated. Ray, standing on the touchline, could stand it no longer. Suddenly, his voice boomed out across the crowd, "Look up, you ----!" Just about every face turned in his direction, and I collapsed with laughter.

When the Riverside Stand was built in 1972 we moved across. Ray liked to sit near the front where he could goad opposing players. On one occasion we were playing Oldham and their left back looked like a man in the twilight of his career. Every time he went near the ball, Ray gave him some terrible stick. The poor man had a nightmare and we murdered them 5–nil. After the game we had a celebratory drink in the players' bar in the Cottage and who did we find ourselves talking to? That's right, our friend from Oldham. "I think I'll be dropped next week," he said. "I've got a wife and four kids at home and I don't know what I'm going to do." After that, I suggested to Ray that in future we might find seats a bit further back.

The move wasn't entirely successful. Fulham were playing in the Anglo-Italian Cup and Ray was enraged when one of their players spat at Freddie Callaghan. "You greasy ----!" shouted my pal, as he leapt out of his seat. Within

Mullers and Raymondo pictured at Craven Cottage in 2012.

seconds, we were surrounded by lots of men who were pointing at Ray and shaking their fists. "Sit down, for God's sake," I said to him. It suddenly dawned on us that we were surrounded by every Italian waiter in London.

As I got to know him better, I realised that all doors opened for Ray Jenkins. We would go to places we should never have been and events we were not invited to. Ray would have a word in the ear of the man on the door and the next minute we'd be in. How he did it, I will never know. If I asked him, he wouldn't tell me but to me Ray Jenkins will always be the man for whom no door was ever closed. In time he became best friends with Freddie Callaghan and Alan Mullery. Freddie and his wife Hazel holiday with the Jenkins every year at their home in Mallorca, and Ray and Alan Mullery once lived in the same road in Banstead and ran a soccer school together.

For me that chance meeting in a bingo hall led to a 40-year friendship full of fun and laughter. Ray is the funniest man not on a stage, and funnier than many who are. Here's a story that illustrates the kind of laughs we've had. We were playing together in a doubles tennis match. Across the net was a boy in his late teens who Ray bollocked for whistling and not taking the game seriously. Bollocking over, Ray then proceeded to serve four consecutive double faults. As each one went in, we were trying desperately not to laugh, but by the time he served the last one, we were all lying on the court clutching our sides. And Ray laughed louder than anyone.

He and Gwen are the most generous hosts anyone could ever meet and, what's more, they introduced me to my future wife, who was Gwen's aerobics teacher. (Ray, the bill is in the post.)

Chapter 7

Early Seventies

Season 1971–72 began with the Whites playing more attractive opposition with the likes of Sheffield Wednesday, Sunderland and a local derby with Queen's Park Rangers, and our season got off to a good start with a 3–nil win against Watford. Then it started to go wrong and the goals dried up. We went six games goalless. We signed Roger Cross, a prolific goalscorer from Brentford, but sadly not destined to be prolific for us. He ran around looking good but rarely managing to find the back of the net.

Mullers came back on loan from Spurs towards the end of the season. He was a player who never gave less than 100 per cent and the punters appreciated him. With his help, we avoided the drop to Division Three, but only just.

In September 1972, a new player made his debut at outside-right. Les Strong wasn't the best right-winger we'd ever seen, but he scored a few vital goals. Manager Alec Stock looked at him and said, "As a right-winger, he'll make a good left back." This was a better season. In the depth of winter we scored 18 goals in 7 matches. At one time we were in with a chance of promotion, but we finished 9th in Division Two.

My own career in radio and television was progressing well and in June 1973 I was offered a three-hour daily afternoon show on Radio One. This set me off on a whirlwind tour of disco appearances around the country – one night Aberdeen, the next Plymouth – and led me to hosting shows like *Top Of the Pops* and *Seaside Special*, but I still managed to get to as many Fulham games as possible.

Les Strong arrives with a smile on his face.

Towards the end of the 1973–74 season Alec Stock persuaded Bobby Moore, the man who had lifted the World Cup at Wembley in 1966, to join Fulham from West Ham and to end his playing career at Craven Cottage. Linking up with Alan Mullery meant that there were two ex-England captains at the Cottage. With Mullers and Mooro as the driving force, Fulham were about to have one of the most outstanding seasons in the club's long history.

Playing the Hamilton Hotshots on Radio One.

Trying to look trendy (!) on Top of the Pops.

Chapter 8

We're Going to Wembley

Season 1974–75 started well enough with a 1–nil win against West Brom and three wins out of the first four games. For almost the only time in their history Manchester United had been relegated to Division Two. A crowd of over 26,000 welcomed them to the Cottage and they beat us 2–1. By January we were into the blood and guts of the FA Cup. In the third round it took us three games to beat Hull City. Back then there were no penalty shoot-outs; matches were replayed until there was a winner. Having at last overcome Hull, we needed four games in Round 4 to beat Nottingham Forest. People started taking us seriously when we won 2–1 away at Everton with a brace from Viv Busby. For the quarter-final we were drawn away at Carlisle, which is as far north as you can go without being in Scotland. But the feeling was – we'd done it at Nottingham Forest, we'd done it at Everton and now we could do it at Carlisle.

It's such a long journey, we decided to fly there. There was Ray Jenkins and his brother Mike and my ten-year-old son, David junior, who, having been born in Manchester, was a Man U fan but had adopted Fulham as his second team. A taxi was booked to pick us up from the airport. It turned out to be an old London black cab, which made us feel at home until we realised it was so old there were holes in the floor and every time it went over a puddle our feet got soaked. There was a lot of laughter and animated conversation about the game to come. We were starting to believe that this could be our year.

Brunton Park, Carlisle, had a lovely setting with sheep grazing in the fields behind one of the stands. It was like a pastoral scene, and with nearly 22,000 packed inside the stadium the atmosphere was white hot. Two Fulham players had absolute blinders. Peter Mellor, the giant blond goalkeeper, had the finest game of his career and Les Barrett tantalised the Carlisle defence, scoring the goal that took us into the semi-finals. After the match we were invited into the dressing room to drink champagne with the players and Tommy Trinder.

In 1975 there was an economy cut at the BBC. The afternoon show on Radio 2 was axed and my show was now broadcast on both Radio 1 and Radio

Don Durbridge, Mike Jenkins and I board the Piper Aztec en route to Manchester for the semi-final replay.

2 giving it a combined audience that the BBC estimated at 16 million. So an awful lot of people were listening as I chronicled Fulham's progress in the FA Cup and they heard some fairly biting remarks I had to make about Birmingham City's Welsh international full-back Malcolm Page and his strong-arm tactics on Les Barrett in the semi-final game at Hillsborough. Johnny Mitchell scored our goal in a 1–all draw so yet another replay was necessary, and this one would be at Maine Road, Manchester, on April 9.

Getting to this game was to cause me great problems. I was on the air at Broadcasting House in London until 5 o'clock and the kick-off in Manchester was at 7.30. There was no public transport that could get me there in time, but there was no way I was going to miss it. I broadcast an SOS on my show a few days before the game, asking if anyone could help. After many calls and lots of negotiations, I finally managed to charter a Piper Aztec. I signed off my show at 5 pm, dashed to Northolt Airport where I met up with the Jenkins brothers and fellow-broadcaster Don Durbridge, who was also the matchday announcer at Fulham. Buzzing with anticipation for the game ahead, we were swiftly airborne and heading for Manchester's Ringway Airport. There we were met by Freddie Pye, an old friend and Manchester City director, who drove us with all speed in his Rolls-Royce to Maine Road. We arrived at the ground just ten minutes after kick-off.

Fortunately, the most important action took place at the end of the match. Ten seconds before the end of extra time the ball hit John Mitchell on the knee and crossed the goal-line. Birmingham were gutted. They just had time to kick off and the referee blew the final whistle. Cue bedlam. We spilled onto the pitch, milling around in a daze. It took time to sink in. After a hundred years Fulham were finally going to Wembley.

In the plane on the way home we enjoyed the champagne we had bought because we knew we were going to make it. There we were, the four of us singing "We're going to Wembley" and wearing the sick bags on our heads as hats. Back in London I raved about it on my radio show. As cup final day grew nearer, I played our own song, *Viva El Fulham* by Tony Rees and the Cottagers. It nudged into the Top 50. The Fulham players were swept off their feet. They were wanted for TV and press interviews and personal appearances and, naturally, they were wondering how much money they could make out of it all. For many of them this was an opportunity that might never come along again.

Just seconds to go – and John Mitchell forces the ball past Birmingham keeper Dave Latchford and over the line for the dramatic winner that takes Fulham to Wembley.

Famous celebrity supporters were swept along with the tide. The *Daily Mirror* photographed musician Alan Price and me along with long-time supporters Honor Blackman and Harry Fowler complete with our Fulham hats and scarves.

But there was still the business of league matches to be played before the big day at Wembley. Three days after the win at Maine Road we were back in Manchester where we lost 1–nil to United at Old Trafford, no disgrace under the circumstances. On April 19, at home to Portsmouth, disaster struck our young left back, Les Strong. 'Strongie', under the careful guidance of Bobby Moore, had turned into a class act. He'd played in every league match of the season and in each of the cup-ties – eleven, incidentally, and the most games any club have ever had to play to reach the cup final. Against Portsmouth he was carried off with a nasty ankle injury. It was touch and go whether he would make it for the big day. Despite a brave effort from this bubbly character, it was not to be. Les lost his battle and through a cruel trick of fate he would have to watch from the sidelines as his colleagues carried the fight to the last round.

As cup final day loomed large, I decided to keep a cup final diary. Entries from the diary are coming up...

I congratulate Mullery and Mitchell in the dressing room at Maine Road.

Tommy Trinder celebrates with match winner John Mitchell.

Chapter 9

Cup Final Diary

MAY 2, 1975

I can't remember when I've looked forward to a weekend more. Tomorrow is the greatest day in Fulham's history. It's taken us more games to get to Wembley than any other team in the history of the FA Cup – eleven altogether, and nearly all away from home. The team, led by the two veterans Moore and Mullery, have played above themselves in every round and we could be forgiven for thinking that our name is on the FA Cup. All the omens look good. Tonight, on the eve of the final, I have two tickets to see David Gates and his band Bread at the Victoria Apollo. Gates sings his songs and the band sounds great, rockier than I had expected. It's a really good concert, the perfect warm-up for the day to follow. The weekend has started well.

As Angie, my girlfriend, and I return to the Rolls-Royce – the obligatory status symbol for a high profile Radio 1 DJ – parked in nearby Vauxhall Bridge Road, we notice it's been scratched. How badly we don't know until I check it in daylight in the morning.

MAY 3, 1975

The day starts badly. As I emerge from my flat in Hallam Street near Broadcasting House I can see that the damage to my car is a lot worse than I thought – a helluva lot. Quite clearly someone has used some instrument, possibly a nailfile, and etched a deep scratch into every single panel of the car – a long, wavy line goes right round every door, the bonnet and the boot. For good measure the vandal has slashed the vinyl roof as well. I don't have a personalised number plate so this is sheer random vandalism. Some bonehead has seen a nice car and set about disfiguring it for no other reason than pure jealousy. It's enough to make anyone weep, and hardly the way to start such a special day.

When Ray Jenkins sees the damage, he does his best to cheer me up. "Don't worry," he says. "It looks as though it's been in a stock car race at Wimbledon." The four of us – the Jenkins brothers, David junior and I – bundle

The cup final squad. Standing: Bill Taylor (coach), Ron Woolnough (physio), Barry Lloyd, Les Strong, John Dowie, John Lacy, Peter Mellor, Ernie Howe, Viv Busby, John Mitchell, John Fraser, John Collins (coach); seated: Jimmy Conway, Alan Slough, captain Alan Mullery, Alec Stock (manager), Bobby Moore, Les Barrett, John Cutbush.

into the car and head for Wembley. I've been to quite a few finals but never when my team is playing.

On the way to the Twin Towers it's clear we're well outnumbered by West Ham supporters, and those who notice it's me at the wheel of the car as we stand in a queue of traffic are smirking and enjoying, as football fans do, the misfortune of someone who supports a rival team. "What a crappy car," I hear one of them shout. "Just like his football team."

"We'll show them," says everyone in the car at the same time.

We're booked for lunch at the Esso Hotel next door to the ground and my embarrassment is compounded when I find I'm parked in the bay next to the

FOOTBALL ASSOCIATION CHALLENGE CUP COMPETITION

FINAL

FULHAM
VERSUS
WEST HAM UNITED

SATURDAY, 3rd MAY, 1975   Kick-off 3 p.m.

Official Souvenir Programme . . . 20p.

EMPIRE WEMBLEY STADIUM

Manager Alec Stock and his West Ham counterpart John Lyall lead out the teams at Wembley. At left holding a walkie-talkie is a security man typically butting into the picture.

Rolls of Gary Glitter, which is in absolutely mint condition. We bolt down our lunch as quickly as we can and head for the ground, eager to find our seats and soak up the atmosphere as early as possible. If you were a Liverpool or a Man United fan, you'd see your team in many cup finals but for us Fulham supporters there's the feeling that this is our once in a lifetime opportunity, and so the team really has to win.

For some reason that I've never fathomed it's the only year there's no community singing and no *Abide With Me* but we don't care. All we care about is that we're here for Fulham's greatest day. Four times previously Fulham have made it as far as the semi-finals. Now at last we're at Wembley and we've done it the hard way with every win away from home. Well, today we're away from home so why shouldn't we win again?

As always on cup final day, the weather is a little muggy with that feeling in the air that the season is changing to summer, but there's a swirling wind that will play havoc with the ball. Some West Ham fans are waving a banner that says 'West Ham 3, Dad's Army 0,' an obvious reference to the veterans, Alan Mullery and Bobby Moore. What a dream day for Bobby to be playing against the team he captained for so long.

At last the teams come out of the tunnel, Fulham led by Alec Stock and West Ham by John Lyall, two of the 'gentleman' managers. The roar of 100,000 spectators is deafening. There's a lump in our throats as we see Les Strong, looking so smart in one of the suits Fulham have bought for the players. Strongie, who did so much to get us to Wembley, is now reduced to being a spectator on what should have been the biggest day of his life.

The match is under way. Fulham quickly settle down, look confident and for the first twenty minutes they're playing the best football. We've already beaten West Ham in the League Cup this season and, though they're in a division above us, we're convinced we can do it again. West Ham are a physically strong side with players like Billy Bonds and Frank Lampard, and Trevor Brooking is the most skilful player on the park, but we're still not bothered. How we shall celebrate tonight if we win!

Big John Lacy – 'Blakey' to the fans – heads just wide, there's a good solo effort and shot from Viv Busby, but that goal just won't come. The only sign of nerves comes from Peter Mellor. Harried and unsettled by Billy Jennings and Alan Taylor, his kicking isn't too good, but Peter has kept twenty clean sheets this season and he, more than anyone, got us to Wembley. We know he won't let us down now.

Half-time comes and it's still goalless. Ray and Mike and David are all happy. They say we've done well. The consensus is that, if anything, we look the better side.

Mullers and Mooro exit Wembley for the last time.

West Ham come out more purposefully after the interval, but Fulham soak up the pressure. When they finally break away John Mitchell has a great shot saved by Mervyn Day. Fifteen minutes into the second half there's a mistake by John Cutbush. Peter Mellor parries Jennings' shot but Alan Taylor pounces on the rebound and almost in slow motion, as Mellor attempts to recover, the ball goes right through his legs into the net.

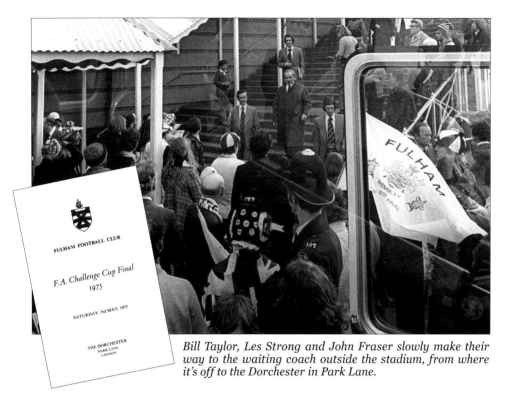

Bill Taylor, Les Strong and John Fraser slowly make their way to the waiting coach outside the stadium, from where it's off to the Dorchester in Park Lane.

We have half an hour left to get the equaliser but now West Ham are getting stronger and more confident. Their fans are singing that song of theirs, *I'm Forever Blowing Bubbles.* I'd like to tell them where to stick their damned bubbles. Four minutes later they've scored their second. Again Peter Mellor has failed to hold a shot and it's that man Alan Taylor who's there to put it away. Two goals in four minutes and the dream is slipping away from us.

Towards the end there's a bit of exhibition stuff, a bit of class from Moore and Mullery and a couple of shots that on another day might have gone in. But by now all we can hear in the stadium is the singing of the West Ham supporters, "We're going to win the cup." With ten minutes to go they're whistling for time and chanting, "Easy, easy." It's not difficult to dislike them. Finally, Pat Partridge, the referee, blows his whistle and puts us out of our suffering. The West Ham players are bounding up the steps to get their medals and Billy Bonds holds the cup aloft. Somehow the legs of the losing team are much more weary. The steps are the final mountain to climb. Tommy Trinder is there, complete with cigar, with a word of consolation, but they hardly hear him. Still, it's been a great occasion for Tommy. Thirty-six years as a director, the last seventeen as chairman and now he's here to see the club's biggest game. As the Hammers do their lap of honour and the band play *Congratulations*, Mooro and Mullers leave the pitch with arms across each other's shoulders. As they approach the tunnel, they applaud the Fulham supporters who in turn applaud them. Between them they will have memories of great triumphs at Wembley but this, we ponder, will surely be the last appearance there for them both. For the others it must be their 'once in a lifetime'. Nothing will ever compare with May 3, 1975. Maybe for us, too.

As they trudge sadly back to the dressing room, Peter Mellor apologises to Alec Stock, "I'm sorry, boss, it was my fault. I should have kept my legs closed."

To which Alec replies drily, "Your mother should have done that years ago."

On the journey home we reflect on what might have been. It was one of the cleanest finals ever, hardly any fouls, not a moment of ill-feeling between the players and not one occasion when a trainer had to come on to the pitch to tend to an injured man. In fact, it upheld the tradition Fulham always had for fair play and good sportsmanship. There were times, too, when we played some beautiful football – a passing game that we had come to expect from an Alec Stock team.

We don't want the day to end and so we drive back to Fulham where the streets are decked out with flags and bunting. All the pubs are packed. Never has a cup final defeat been so celebrated. We end up in the Half Way House in Lillie Road where we are mobbed by Fulham fans. The place is heaving and to get away Ray Jenkins carries me out on his shoulders. It's only the next morning that we wake up and it finally sinks in that we lost it. But what the hell? All that really matters is that we were there. How Fulhamish is that?

Chapter 10

This is Your Life

Writing in Fulham's souvenir brochure after the game, Alec Stock said, "There can be no doubt that 1975 was the best year in Fulham's history. We reached Wembley, our skipper Alan Mullery was named Footballer of the Year and our chairman Tommy Trinder rounded it all off by being awarded the CBE. What makes Fulham different is that we do things properly and proudly. We don't fall out with our rivals, we don't set out to beat them at all costs, by trickery or tough methods. We remember our dignity and the people we are there to entertain."

Tommy Trinder wrote: "The dancing in the streets around Craven Cottage was something to behold. In the end the achievement of getting there, against all the odds, of being only the seventh second division side to make it, became something worth celebrating. That most human and excellent of managers Alec Stock made sure we did it the Fulham way, too. Every one of our players was a credit to the club and his profession, and throughout our cup run we offered an image of soccer that was refreshing and wholesome."

Sadly, as we shall see, it would not be long before Mullery, Stock and Trinder would all be gone from the club. After the cup there was always going to be an anti-climax and on January 3, 1976, we were knocked out of the competition at the first attempt, beaten 3–2 at home by Huddersfield in the third round. We finished the season halfway up the league. More significantly, Alan Mullery decided to retire at the end of the season. The knocks and bumps he'd had over the years had taken their toll. The doctor told him that if he played on, he would regret it later in life. The club said they would give him a testimonial in view of the two spells he had at Fulham, at the beginning and end of his career. We reflected on what a fighter he was, a captain who drove on the players around him, and remembered some of the great goals he scored, like the absolute scorcher from 25 yards against Leicester.

MARCH 1976
The phone rang at my flat in Hallam Street and Mullers was on the line. "I'm

Alan Mullery receives a tankard from chairman Tommy Trinder to mark the skipper's 400th game for the club in December 1975.

organising my testimonial," he said. "I've got the England World Cup squad from 1966 to play an ex-Fulham XI. A couple of the World Cup team can't make it, and rather than ask a couple of other pros, I thought I'd invite you and Jimmy Tarbuck to play. How do you fancy it?" Resisting the temptation to say, "Unfortunately, I'm busy that evening" (oh, yeah), I put down the phone in a state of shock. The boy who never made it as a pro was now invited to play with the England World Cup team. Wow! Dreams do come true after all.

The big night came along and there I was getting changed in the dressing room at Craven Cottage with the greatest team of all time. What do you say at a time like that? Not much, is the answer. Just keep your mouth shut and listen. The *Fulham Chronicle* said it all on March 26 and gave me a press cutting I have cherished for life: *England scored first when Jack Charlton gave a fine ball to David Hamilton who crossed for brother Bobby to rocket it into the top of the net.*

After the match Jimmy Tarbuck and I were filmed paying our personal tributes to Alan Mullery. Mullers didn't know it yet but he was about to get captured by Eamonn Andrews and the famous red book for *This Is Your Life*. Eamonn crept up on him in the dressing room. "What a relief," said Alan afterwards. "All those whispered calls June, my wife, had been having. For ages I was convinced she was having an affair."

Many people thought Mullers would be Alec Stock's eventual successor, including Alan himself, but the appointment of Bobby Campbell in the summer of '76 put an end to that and Alan got his first managerial break at Brighton. Wherever he went in the future, he wouldn't be forgotten at Craven Cottage. One fan made sure of that. He (or maybe she...) whitewashed a message on the wall opposite the Stevenage Road stand which would stay there for many years. It said: 'MULLERY IS GOD'.

Chapter 11

Les Barrett

Not long after Mullers retired, another stalwart from the cup final team moved on. Les Barrett went to Millwall. He didn't want to. If he'd previously turned down Manchester United and Tottenham, he certainly didn't want to play for Millwall. The only team he ever wanted to play for was Fulham, but he was coming towards the end of his career, all he'd ever done was play football and this was a move he got talked into. In 1976 Les was awarded a testimonial for ten sterling years at Fulham. I was elected chairman of his testimonial committee. The treasurer was Tom Tonkin, a lovely old boy. He and his wife Maud were a driving force behind the scenes at the club. The other committee members were my pals Alex Shooter and Ray Jenkins, Peter Tyers, the sports editor of the *Fulham Chronicle*, and Dennie and Len Mancini, the brothers from the boxing world, whose sports shop was a fixture in the Fulham Palace Road.

Tom Tonkin, proudly sporting his Fulham tie.

For the main match Fulham were pitched against their old rivals from Wembley, West Ham, and for the warm-up game I put together an All Star XI to play against an ex-Fulham XI. The stars were all keen to play at Craven Cottage and to turn out for Les, and we ran out with a line-up that included actors Dennis Waterman, Patrick Mower and Richard O'Sullivan – all in big series at the time – comedian Peter Cook and rock star Rick Wakeman. For me, it was the second chance to play on the hallowed turf in a year. Later I played in two more testimonials, for Les Strong and Gordon Davies.

TEAMCHECK

EX·FULHAM

ALL STAR XI

EX·FULHAM		ALL STAR XI
MALCOLM WEBSTER	1	JESS CONRAD *Pop singer*
KEN CRAGGS	2	DENNIS WATERMAN *from TV's 'The Sweeney'*
JIM LANGLEY	3	MICHAEL WALE *Pop music writer & 'Today' interviewer*
ALAN MULLERY	4	RICHARD O'SULLIVAN *TV's 'Man about the House'*
BILL DODGIN	5	MICHAEL REDFERN *actor and staunch Fulham supporter*
STAN BROWN	6	PETER COOK *'Pete and Dud' fame*
BERNARD NEWCOMBE	7	DAVID HAMILTON *Radio 1 DJ*
JIMMY HILL	8	PATRICK MOWER *from TV's 'Special Branch'*
STEVE EARLE	9	RICK WAKEMAN *Top rock star*
PAT O'CONNELL	10	TONY SELBY *from TV's 'Get Some In'*
TOSH CHAMBERLAIN	11	ROBIN ASQUITH *Star of 'Confessions of a .....' films*
	12	ROY NORTH *from TV's 'Basil Brush Show'*
	13	PETER BRABROOKE *Former Chelsea & West Ham player*

REFEREE: C Downey (Middlesex)
LINESMEN: Red flag – P Tyers (Fulham Chronicle); Yellow flag – M Ford (West London Observer)

COMMENTATORS: DON DURBRIDGE & ROGER KITTER

As a member of the Showbiz XI, I played on lots of league grounds but nothing beats playing on the pitch of the team you support and alongside the players who are your heroes but also have become your friends.

The lethal right foot (!) in Les's testimonial game.

Chapter 12

Bestie and Marsh

Everybody loved to play for Alec Stock. The man who persuaded Alan Mullery to come back and Bobby Moore to move from his beloved West Ham worked his magic again at the start of the 1976–77 season when he wooed George Best and Rodney Marsh to the Cottage. Both had been playing in the USA, Best with Los Angeles Aztecs and Marsh with Tampa Bay Rowdies. With Mooro still at the club, three of the biggest names in soccer were at Fulham, albeit at the end of their careers. In the short term, it was a good way of solving Fulham's dwindling gates. A crowd of 21,000 turned up to see Bestie score in his first game. That one goal was enough to beat Bristol Rovers. But the game we'll never forget was on September 25, 1976, when Fulham thrashed Hereford United 4–1 in the late summer sunshine. They were so much on top and Best and Marsh were so keen to get the ball that they tackled each other, although they were on the same side. It was pure showboating, the crowd loved it and the clip of that famous tackle was shown again and again on television. We all

The TV line-up caption for the memorable game at home to Hereford.

Hereford try to get to grips with mercurial George Best whilst Rodney Marsh looks on, perhaps wondering whether to tackle his team-mate.

headed home after the game having had a thoroughly uplifting afternoon by the river. If Fulham weren't going to win anything, at least they were going to be the 'entertainers', and maybe that wasn't such a bad thing.

Sadly, it didn't last too long. Things started to go wrong when the pitches got heavier. Peter Mellor got a nasty injury in the 5–1 home defeat by Notts County in November and Fulham signed a new goalkeeper, Gerry Peyton, ironically from Mellor's old club, Burnley. It was Peter's last game for the club and he was transferred to Hereford. It was sad to say goodbye to a man who more than anyone had got us to Wembley and who for me had become a personal friend.

Worse was to come. In December in an amazing boardroom coup Tommy Trinder resigned as chairman and Alec Stock was replaced by Bobby Campbell. Less than two years after the great cup run both Trinder and Stock had been toppled. We supporters just couldn't understand it. We knew the club had financial troubles and that many of them stemmed from the cost of building the riverside stand in 1972. A man who had much to do with that was Eric

Miller, managing director of Peachey Property Corporation, an Arsenal supporter who, unable to acquire a place on the board at Highbury, had become a director at Fulham. Sir Eric, as he became, having been knighted by Harold Wilson, was brought in by Tommy Trinder to help the club's finances and was joined on the board by his friend, the Yorkshire businessman Ernie Clay.

On the pitch, under Bobby Campbell's guidance, things were not going well. Relegation was on the cards, but late signings of Ray Evans, a tough tackling full-back from Millwall and Peter Storey, the Arsenal wing-half, helped us avoid the drop – two tough guys who gave the team a bit of steel.

Alec Stock, receiving a Manager of the Month award, was wise enough not to attempt a Seventies hairstyle!

George Best always wanted to play for Chelsea. He reckoned that as he'd done most of his best work in the Kings Road, this was the natural place for him to be. I suppose for Bestie Fulham was the next best thing, if you'll pardon the pun. Local derbies between Fulham and Chelsea were always something special. At Christmas 1976, my pals and I were among a crowd of over 55,000 who saw Chelsea beat the Whites 2–nil at Stamford Bridge. Micky Droy kicked Bestie all over the park.

By this time my daughter, Jane, had started going to home matches and would sit next to Bestie's wife, Angie. Angie was constantly enraged with referees who she felt didn't give George enough protection. The trouble was George had lost his pace and defenders were catching him. Players who wouldn't have lived with him years before were now taking great pleasure out of clogging a legend. Angie told us that after a match his legs were covered in bruises. Angie spent most of the match hurling abuse at the ref and Jane, who was going to a school that turned out young ladies, was learning a whole new vocabulary.

Revenge is sweet. Chelsea came to the Cottage in April 1977 and we won 3–1 with goals by Alan Warboys, John Mitchell and... George Best. I bet he enjoyed that one.

Bobby Moore opened his new bar, Mooro's, in Stratford and invited me along to do the opening night disco. Les Strong was there, the champagne flowed and a good night was had by all. Bobby retired at the end of the season.

Elton John was said to want him as manager at Watford but it didn't transpire and Graham Taylor got the job. Why didn't anyone realise that such a great player could make a good manager? It's one of the mysteries of football. And here's another. Boardroom coup number 2 at Fulham. Almost the entire board resigned, including Tommy Trinder who had been made life president. Obviously, life president means as much as life imprisonment. Once again we Fulhamites were baffled. How could a man who loved the club so much, who basked in the reflected glory of 1975, now leave with barely a whimper? Was there something we hadn't been told? There were rumours, of course, but personally I never heard the answer.

In September on the Jewish Day of Atonement Sir Eric Miller committed suicide. He was the subject of an enquiry by the Fraud Squad. Before the case came to court, he blew his brains out. His shareholding was taken over by Ernie Clay, who became the club's new chairman and, in his friend's honour, he renamed the Riverside Stand the Eric Miller Stand. Thus began the most turbulent period in the club's history and one that very nearly spelt the end of Craven Cottage.

Chapter 13

Edward

There are football supporters and there are Fulham supporters. The two are quite different. Anyone growing up in south-west London or Surrey in the 1970s would almost certainly gravitate to Chelsea. People tend to follow a winning team, and the Blues had done their share of winning. With Peter Osgood, Alan Hudson and 'Chopper' Harris they were the self-styled 'Kings of the Kings Road'.

Not much more than a mile separates the grounds of Chelsea and Fulham and yet the clubs and their supporters are poles apart. It would take a certain type of person to follow a quirky sort of club that has what looks like a cricket pavilion on one of its corners and a listed stand that harks back to days long gone.

Edward Burston was a Fulham supporter. Actually, that understates it. He was fanatical about the club. He was a wealthy man, though you wouldn't know it to look at him. He was a small, shy man who sat almost nervously in the Riverside Stand. You wouldn't notice him in the crowd were it not for the fact that sitting next to him was his beautiful Japanese girlfriend, Emico. They lived together in his penthouse flat overlooking Hyde Park and by one of those extraordinary ironies in life Edward was born on the day the Japanese bombed Pearl Harbour. Apart from Emi, Fulham was his great passion. He frequently invited me to dinner at his flat where he showed me Fulham videos and talked endlessly about the club and the team. He never let me leave without giving me a memento, usually a Fulham shirt. Eventually, I had enough shirts to start my own team.

One evening we went to dinner at the Japanese restaurant in the Kensington Hilton Hotel. Edward was worried. Because he had money Fulham wanted him to become a director. He wasn't typical director material. He didn't like attention and publicity, but he would do anything to help the club. By becoming a director he would have to lend the club £25,000. That was a drop in the ocean to him, but he had a deep distrust of the chairman, Ernie Clay. "He has no love of Fulham," Edward said to me over dinner. "He comes from

Huddersfield, likes rugby. What's he doing here?" Edward was convinced that Clay had only one interest in Fulham. "He has seen the ground as a prime site for redevelopment," he said. "There is a block of flats next door where

penthouses sell at £250,000. Imagine the value of sixty of those on Craven Cottage." Edward was also sceptical of the suicide of Sir Eric Miller. "How can a man kill himself by putting two bullets through his own brain?" I pondered what he meant. Did he think someone wanted him out of the way before the Fraud Squad enquiry?

"What we need," said Edward, "is a board full of genuine Fulham supporters who will make sure this remains a football club, not businessmen who see the ground as a potential crock of gold. We need people like yourself."

I must say at this point I'd never seen myself as a football club director. I remember the book by the legendary Len Shackleton which had a chapter headed 'What The Average Director Knows About Football'. Underneath was a blank page. That's how it was in Len's day. But Edward was convincing and taking the point that it would need real Fulham supporters to save the club, I warmed to the idea. The only problem was I had just gone through an expensive divorce. Having said goodbye to my house, I was in the process of buying another one in Barnes and I didn't have a spare £25,000 that I could invest in the club. Burston was determined and arranged a meeting with Ernie Clay. He told Clay he would become a director on condition that I would join him on the board. He explained that I couldn't put money in but said I would raise money for the club by doing discos and arranging pop concerts.

Ernie Clay

Clay phoned me and asked me to go and see him at his sumptuous home in Betchworth. He was what you might call a 'character', a big, blunt Yorkshireman with a thick neck and a crew-cut. His wife, Marie, by contrast, was a quiet, charming lady. Beauty and the Beast, I thought.

"We understand about the money, we understand you're skint," said Clay in that caustic way of his. "But Edward wants you on the board and I've agreed with him." A few days later I was in the office at Craven Cottage writing out a cheque for one hundred one-pound shares, which every board member had to do, and the *Evening Standard* on July 18, 1978, ran the headline: 'Hamilton On Fulham Board'. I have to say it was pretty exciting – becoming a director of the club I'd supported since I was a boy. I was determined to help in any way I could and, bearing in mind Edward's fears, one way I would try to help was in making sure Craven Cottage continued to be a football ground.

Not long afterwards, Edward was caught up in a drama he could have done without. For some time I'd had a much publicised affair with the model and page 3 girl Kathy McKinnon. Kathy's father was a High Court judge and every time he presided over a controversial case the newspapers would dig out a photo of Kathy and there would usually be a mention of me. We became each other's publicity machine. Kathy and I had lived together for four years, although it didn't seem that long as I was always working, doing my daily radio show, hosting Top Of The Pops or doing gigs around the country. Probably largely because of the pressure of work, we had decided to go our separate ways. Word got out and the press camped out on the doorstep of my new home in Ranelagh Avenue, Barnes. When Edward arrived to have one of his many chats about Fulham, he found himself surrounded by paparazzi. An hour later when it was time to leave for my radio show, there were even more there. "Come on, I'll get you out of this," said Edward. We leapt out of the house into his open top Porsche and zoomed off up the road. The best the photographers could do was get a shot of the back of his car. As the dust settled, the number plate became clear. It read... FU 2.

My first match as a director was the opening game of the new season at Bristol Rovers. I went to it with my friend and fellow-supporter Alex Shooter. I'd first met Alex at Fulham in the mid-Seventies and we immediately became best buddies. There's always a feeling of expectancy at the start of a new season and it's always good to start with a win under your belt. Sadly for us, this was not the case. We'd signed a player from the reserve team at Plymouth called Geoff Banton. As Banton struggled in the sunshine at Eastville, Clay turned to us directors and said, "See 'im? 'Eel play for England one day."

"I don't think so," said Alex. "I don't think he can play." Sometimes people from Northern Ireland can be as blunt as those from Yorkshire.

The programme for the home game against Burnley in August 1978 announces that I'm the latest addition to the board, joining chairman Ernie Clay, his son Gregory, Edward Burston, Brian Dalton (the club's accountant), David Peters (Eric Miller's son-in-law) and Alan Price. The programme notes also announce that in the first of a series of fundraising discos I am bringing fellow DJ Tony Blackburn from Radio 1 to the Cottage for a show in the Riverside Suite on August 31.

On August 31 Blackburn played to a full house, raising lots of money for the club.

Up for the cup. Alex Shooter, Les Strong and me.

Chapter 14

Strongie

I did several disco nights at the club. Often the players came along and had a good time and we became good friends. Les Strong is a funny man, a natural storyteller. He even played the game with a smile on his face. He told me the story of one of his colleagues, a hard man on the pitch, but not very successful with women. Les told it like this...

"Halfway through a dance, women walk off the floor because of his bad language. We've tried to tell him women don't like hearing a load of bad language when they're dancing and if he wants to get anywhere with them, he needs to cut it out. He assures us that this is what he'll do but at the next club function the same thing happens. As he strolls back to the bar somebody says, 'There you are, you've done it again.' 'Not at all,' he says. 'I remembered what you said about not swearing and I couldn't think of a thing to say so to break the ice I just said, "You don't sweat much for a fat girl, do you?"'"

Under Bobby Moore's guidance, Les turned into a really good player. There was even talk of him playing for England. George Best wasn't such a good influence. We had a 12 o'clock kick-off at Crystal Palace and beat them 3–2 in a hard local derby. Having a drink with Les at the bar after the game, I complimented him on his performance. "That's interesting," said Les, "because Bestie and I were out on the piss last night. We didn't go to bed all night and, to be honest, we were still pissed when we kicked off at 12 o'clock."

"Well," I said. "If you can play like that on a Saturday afternoon, maybe you should make that your training schedule on a Friday night."

From the picture album

The Radio 1 line-up in the Seventies. Standing, left to right: Jimmy Savile, Ed Stewart, Dave Lee Travis, Emperor Rosko, Alan Freeman, Anne Nightingale, John Peel, Johnnie Walker and Terry Wogan. Front: DH, Noel Edmonds and Tony Blackburn.

From the picture album

The Welsh team drop in on my gig at the Valbonne Club.

Fulham's great Welshman Gordon 'Ivor' Davies celebrates one of his 178 goals for the club.

Chapter 15

From a Director's Diary

SEPTEMBER 2, 1978

On my way to West Ham in my Mini, the car breaks down a few miles short of the ground. I'm standing by it when a young man in a black and white scarf pulls up and offers to help. I tell him if he'll give me a lift to the ground, he can park in my space in the directors' car park. Sounds like a good deal. The young man is David Roodyn, off to the match with his friend, Nick. Thus is formed another Fulham friendship that will last for many years. David is a lawyer who gives the club much legal advice, and writes many distinctive columns for the club's programme. Another passionate fan who could only choose Fulham as his club.

With the Diddymobile – and with David Roodyn, connoisseur of football and ladies. I hosted David's 50th birthday party at the Arts Club in Piccadilly, a night of merriment and mirth. Today he runs the 1879 Club for Fulham supporters which meets once a quarter. Our chairman is the patron, and guest interviewees have included Chris Coleman, Roy Hodgson, Ray Lewington and George Cohen. David is also part of the Locale lunch club in Munster Road, along with Peter Jacobs, Stephen Lewis and Trevor Williams.

After the West Ham game I bump into my boyhood hero, Sam Bartram, now a sports writer with the *Sunday People*. He gives me a nice mention in his column the next day. How the wheel turns full circle. Twenty years ago I was writing about him in *Soccer Star*.

OCTOBER 14, 1978
We lose 3–nil at Brighton. Alan Mullery, Brighton's manager, emerges triumphantly at the end of the game. What could be sweeter than victory over his old club? "Two things I have to take you to task about," says Mullers over a drink in his office. "You're always mentioning Fulham on the radio and [nodding at Alan Price] you're always playing his records."

"You have to look after your own, Mullers," I say.

Three months later in a match against Sunderland Alan Price is in the directors' box wearing a red and white scarf. Twice when Sunderland score he jumps out of his seat. Funny behaviour for a Fulham director.

JANUARY 31, 1979
The highlight of our season, and 25,000 turn up to see us play Manchester United in the FA Cup. It's great to see one of the big clubs back at Craven Cottage. Sadly, United equalise when the ball hits Tony Gale on the bottom and ricochets into the

A very youthful Tony Gale.

back of the net. Galey had made his Fulham debut three years earlier at the age of 16. He looked like one of those players who was going to be too good for the club to hang on to. We'll forgive him for today's bum note.

SEPTEMBER 8, 1979
Away at Queen's Park Rangers. Tony Currie hits a screamer from 25 yards that rockets into the top of the net. I turn to Ernie Clay. "Now that's class," I say.

"Rubbish," says Clay. "It could have gone anywhere in the ground." The fact that it didn't is good enough for QPR. They win 3–nil.

Chapter 16

Sayonara at the Orient

In 1979 the club is the subject of an FA enquiry into illegal payment of players. The incident goes back to the regime before the current board but if any mud hits the fan it could look bad for us. Edward Burston and I ask to see the club's books. Clay refuses. "But we're directors," says Burston, "and we must be able to see the accounts." "You can't," says Clay, and that's that. Burston and I withdraw to consider our positions. I'm working under contract to the BBC and can't afford bad publicity. Burston is becoming increasingly distrustful of Clay. "He's desperately getting hold of every share he can," says Edward. "Why? Who would want thousands of shares in a penniless football club?" Relations between myself and Clay are becoming strained. Once I regarded him as a 'character', but now his bombastic attitude is beginning to grate. It's clear the club is run by one man and the rest of the board are just there to make up the numbers. Maybe Burston is right and Clay has a hidden agenda. I don't like the way things are going and, weighing up all the circumstances, feel that the best outcome is for me to resign.

Clay demands I return my one hundred one-pound shares. Burston says Clay is desperate for every share he can lay his hands on and suspects it's because he wants complete control of the club so he can sell the ground for redevelopment. So I dig my heels in. "You show me in writing where it says I have to give back the shares," I tell Clay, "and then I'll give them back." Clay leaves a message on my answerphone saying that if I don't return the shares, he will do something that could be harmful to my career.

I'm in shock. We're talking 100 shares here, and for this he makes a threat! I check my cupboard for skeletons. There aren't any, but if someone starts saying dreadful things about you, there's always somebody who's prepared to believe them, particularly if the person saying it happens to be the chairman of a famous football club. For the sake of £100 worth of shares, it isn't worth it. Better to go quietly, like Tommy Trinder.

I agree to give back the shares at the away game at Orient. It's my last match as a director, and the Winstone family who run Leyton Orient have laid

- 77 -

on a wonderful spread in the boardroom. "F-----g 'ell," bellows Clay as he walks in. "Is there a decent fish and chip shop round here?"

The Orient board are lovely, friendly people. "Any time you want to come to our matches, you'll be very welcome," says Brian Winstone, the chairman. "But do me a favour. [Nodding in the direction of Clay...] Don't bring him with you."

Fulham lose the game at Orient 1–nil on what is a fairly miserable afternoon. From the middle of December they go thirteen games without a win. At the end of a wretched season the club is relegated. As someone who is no longer on the board, I am unable to help. But the truth is, I was powerless anyway. The club under Clay is run by one man. He's grabbing as many shares as he can for whatever reason that may become apparent in the future.

Next season we'll be in Division Three. Whichever division we're in, I'll be there watching. This is my club, the one I chose when I was nine. I was there long before Clay and I'll be there long after he's gone. Providing there's still a club to come to.

From now on I'll enjoy watching the games purely as a supporter, without having to worry about how the club is run. During my time as a director I've not taken a penny from the club. I've done several shows for nothing and not even charged travelling expenses to go to away matches. I'm not sure the same could be said about Ernie Clay.

More than ever Edward Burston is convinced that Clay wants to sell the ground for development. "One day," says Edward, looking down at the pitch, "this will be one huge block of flats."

Chapter 17

More Fun Playing

Playing football is much more fun. By the late Seventies I'm playing for three teams. Most Sundays there's a game with the Showbiz XI. Alex Shooter and I join a team called the Happy Wanderers. It's a team of mainly Fulham supporters run by Peter Tyers, sports editor of the Fulham Chronicle. Tosh Chamberlain plays for us and scores an average of about four a game. He still

has the hardest kick in football. He's a great guy, very funny and a pleasure to play alongside. Whereas the Showbiz XI's matches are all over the country, the Happy Wanderers play nearer home so after a busy working week there's not so much travelling involved on a Sunday. Peter Mellor comes along to referee some of our matches and is particularly interested in the form of Tyers, the goalkeeper, who's known as 'The Flying Pig' because of his ample size. At one match Mellor is doubled up with laughter. "What happened?" I ask. "It's the flying pig," he says. "He just dived for the ball. He missed it but he caught his cap."

Peter Mellor checks my boots before a game.

I've also been asked to captain the Radio One football team. They've asked me because, apart from John Peel, no-one else is much interested in football or plays the game. Because of the publicity that the games are given on air, huge crowds turn up for our matches. Sunderland are in the second division and when we go to Roker Park we draw the biggest crowd they've had there all season. We're in the dressing room in the Sunderland kit when the controller of Radio One

The Commentators XI hit Florida. Line-up includes Denis Law, Ian St John, John Motson, Fulham boys Peter Mellor and Teddy Maybank, Roger Hunt, Alan Parry, Jim Rosenthal and Martin Tyler.

strolls in and demands we change into Radio One T-shirts. His assistant, a football man (and Crystal Palace supporter) insists we stay as we are. Peel and I know he's right. After a long verbal battle, he wins the day and we run out in the red and white strip to a huge welcome from the Wearsiders' fans, especially as we're playing against Radio Newcastle in their familiar black and white. Luckily, we win the match.

Next stop, Old Trafford. Huge crowds are outside as the Radio One coach pulls up at the famous stadium. I have to admit I'm feeling pretty nervous, especially as one of the opposing team is the great Bobby Charlton. Once the game has started it's clear that although he retired a few years ago, Bobby is still super-fit, still has plenty of pace and still has that rocket shot. Midway through the first half he takes an in-swinging corner kick with his right foot and places it over the goalkeeper into the roof of the net. Someone unwisely mentions something about 'fluke'. "You think it was a fluke, do you?" says Bobby. Later in the game he scores again direct from a corner kick, this time with his left foot. And this time nobody mentions the word 'fluke'.

In 1981 I go with the Commentators XI for a two-week trip, including four matches, to Tampa Bay, Florida. The team is a mixture of broadcasters including John Motson, Martin Tyler, Alan Parry and Jim Rosenthal and ex-pros like Denis Law, Ian St John, Roger Hunt and Teddy Maybank. My room-mate for the trip is Peter Mellor. We are the Fulham boys, also known as the Little and Large Show.

As you might imagine, seventeen blokes on an unsupervised football trip to Florida is a recipe for a fairly wild time. Some of the matches are fairly tough, notably one against a team from Cuba who for some reason want to go to war with the Brits and have two men sent off in a 'friendly'.

There is one match in which I am definitely the 'fall guy'. It is decided that we will change at our hotel and travel by coach to the ground. As we are about to leave, the area is hit by a giant thunderstorm. I'm in the lift travelling down to the ground floor when suddenly there is a power failure. The lift grinds to a halt between floors. Slowly the lights go out, then the air conditioning goes off. It's getting hotter and hotter and feeling more and more claustrophobic, and

Tommy Steele and I (left in front row) line up in front of Johnny Haynes (at second left) for a charity match at Charlton's ground, The Valley. Playing with the Maestro – it doesn't get any better than that.

the thought is going through my mind, "Does anyone know I'm in here?" I bang on the doors, but nothing happens. Gradually, I sink to the floor, bathed in a pool of perspiration and almost unconscious. Suddenly, the doors open and there in the reception area is a huge crowd of people gaping at the sight of this English 'footballer' crumpled in a heap on the floor. Not exactly the best preparation for a match!

It's on this trip that Peter Mellor decides he loves Florida so much that he will emigrate there with his wife and family. He does so, and in time becomes goalkeeping coach for the USA soccer team.

Chapter 18

Bobby Campbell and Malcolm Macdonald

Back home Bobby Campbell is Fulham's manager. No doubt under Ernie Clay's orders, he's selling players and making money. Ray Evans goes to Stoke City for £120,000, John Lacy to Spurs for £200,000, Ernie Howe to QPR for £50,000, Viv Busby to Norwich for £50,000, Les Barrett to Millwall for £12,000, Perry Digweed to Brighton for £150,000 and Richard Money to Liverpool for £333,333. He's also sold the walking wounded – Chris Guthrie to Millwall for £100,000, though he hardly plays a game, and there's a court battle between the clubs over the transfer fee. Teddy Maybank is sold twice, to Brighton for £237,000 and to PSV Eindhoven in Holland for £250,000. Unfortunately, if you get rid of all your assets, the result is almost certainly going to be relegation which is why, just five years after their greatest day at Wembley, Fulham find themselves in Division Three.

Bobby Campbell

Two new players do come in and turn out to be bargain buys. £50,000 is spent on a battling midfielder who might have a good future at Fulham: Ray Lewington. And just £4,000 paid to Merthyr Tydfil secures the services of Gordon Davies, about as good a bit of business as Fulham will ever do.

In 1980 Bobby Campbell leaves, to be replaced by the club's commercial

Ivor gets his Man of the Match award.

- 83 -

The most famous balcony scene since Romeo and Juliet. Fulham players celebrate promotion on the balcony of the Cottage after the Lincoln game. Note that Les Strong is the one drinking the champagne.

manager and former player, Malcolm Macdonald. The following season, under Malcolm, the team is promoted. Promotion is won with a nervous draw at home to Lincoln in the last match of the season, big Roger Brown our centre back scoring our vital goal. By one point we go up and Lincoln don't. The players celebrate with champagne on the balcony of the Cottage.

1981 is a good year for me. ITV ask me to host a prime-time Saturday night light entertainment show called *Up For The Cup*. It's a talent show with a difference. All the acts are representing football clubs, many of which have their own social club at which these acts might appear; it's run on a knock-out basis and the judges are famous footballers, among them Malcolm Macdonald, so plenty of gags about Fulham. Two of the acts go on to greater success. Bobby Davro makes his debut on the show and Jim Bowen goes on to host the long-running game show *Bullseye*. His catchphrase is 'smashing, lovely'. Jim later admits he's so nervous in the early editions and so caught up in the mechanics of the game that he doesn't always catch what the contestants say. He asks one man what he does for a living. "I'm out of work, Jim," comes the reply, to which Jim replies, "Smashing, lovely." There but for the grace of God…

It's Les Strong's testimonial season and, as with Les Barrett, I'm invited to be on the committee running it. There's a wild night at a pub in Sheen where someone (not me!) has arranged a stripper. She gets one of our gang up on stage, undresses him and starts to get him at it. Unfortunately, he's had a skinful and fails to rise to the occasion. In a promotion season when the Fulham chant has been "Going up, going up, going up," the entire room now starts singing, "Going down, going down, going down." Once again, there but for the grace of God...

We nearly make it two promotions in a row in 1982–83. In the early part of the season the goals are fairly rattling in for Gordon Davies and Dean Coney. Fulham fans particularly take Davies to their hearts. He isn't the biggest striker we'll ever have but his wholehearted performances and his ability to hit the back of the net earn him the nickname 'Ivor', as in Ivor the Engine. Ivor plays to the crowd and thus begins a mutual love-in between him and the Fulham faithful.

Malcolm Macdonald

In the second half of the season Coney mislays his goalscoring boots. Andy Thomas comes in on loan from Oxford United, looks good and scores a couple of goals. Clay could buy him for £30,000, an outlay that could help us back into the top division, but he won't spend the money. In the end we're denied promotion by one point when, in a game we need to win at Derby, the crowd invade the pitch and the game is abandoned two minutes before the end. The FA refuse to let the game be re-played, the result, a 1–nil defeat, stands and Leicester get promotion instead. It leaves a bad taste all round. We are all left very angry and frustrated – frustrated at the authorities and also with Clay for not doing more when we were so close to returning to the big time. There was a strong feeling that he didn't want promotion.

The following season Clay sacks Malcolm Macdonald, apparently because of things that were going on in his private life – scant reward for his success on the field.

From the picture album

DJ's night out – Chris Tarrant, Russ
Williams and Tony Blackburn give
me a leg up.

Chapter 19

Strongie – International Manager

Les Strong made 427 appearances for Fulham, putting him in the top ten of appearances by a Fulham player. When the end came, it came suddenly and while he was still quite young. Having captained the promotion-winning team of 1981–82, he played three games at the start of the next season. Of those three games, Fulham won one and drew two and conceded only two goals, and yet for the next game he was replaced by Kevin Lock. That's football, I suppose some might say. At the age of 29 such a popular player was finished at the club he loved after giving it years of loyal service. He played a few games at Brentford and Crystal Palace and one at Rochdale before hanging up his boots, but he was never really happy anywhere else. He told me that when he retired he didn't miss the game that much. For a while he ran a pub in Richmond although on many days he was out on the golf course.

Les never let business get in the way of pleasure. "What if, while you're out, the staff have their fingers in the till?" I asked him. "If they do, they do," said Les philosophically. "I'd rather be out playing golf than hanging around keeping an eye on them."

Where many of today's footballers don't seem to develop a personality until they get to 30, Les was a 'character' long before that with his ready sense of humour and his eye for the ladies. During his playing days we were great pals and he, of course, was also pals with George Best. Bestie grew a beard, so Les grew a beard. Then I grew a beard as well, though I swiftly shaved it off after an appearance on *Blankety Blank* when the Bromley Townswomen's Guild wrote in to say that I looked sinister. Sinister, indeed!

Tired of being a pub landlord, Les ran the catering at Fulham for a while. He was one of the few people who got on with Ernie Clay, with whom he enjoyed a cheeky repartee. After a world tour with his pal Ron Hetherington, a hard-drinking Fulham supporter, Les decided to move to the USA. Ron had a factory in Fulham and one night Les and I were at a party there when a mass fight

I gave Les the fanzine in Anguilla because I know there are two things that he loves – sitting in the sun and reading about himself.

Les in paradise. On a Caribbean beach with four girls (including Mrs H, second right).

broke out. People were picking up chairs and cracking each other over the head with them. "I don't fancy this, do you?" said Les.

"Not my game," I said, so we legged it out of the back door. We are convinced to this day that we were the only two people there who didn't get involved in the brawl.

Once Les was settled in the States, he started looking for work and, since I was working at the BBC, he asked if I would send a letter recommending he get a green card (which would enable him to work). I sent a serious one, but also enclosed a spoof one which I knew would make him laugh. In the spoof one I wrote: "Please give Les Strong a green card – it will add to the large collection he already has of red and yellow ones."

Les's next stop was Anguilla, a small British island in the Caribbean. It was there that Alex Shooter married his girlfriend, Kim, on a desert island a couple of miles off the coast that had nothing but a few palm trees and a bar. I flew over to be his best man. Peter Mellor flew in from America as another guest. Anguilla was the ideal honeymoon location – quiet, sparsely populated, warm the whole year round with lots of sandy beaches and so crime-free that you could leave your door unlocked at night.

It was such an idyllic setting for a wedding that I decided I would marry my girlfriend, Dreena, there a couple of years later. The only problem was the wedding had to be secret because it was being paid for by *Hello* magazine. On the day of the wedding Les rang me at the hotel to tell me he'd organised a football match in the afternoon featuring the local football team and inviting me to the match. It was at the same time that we were getting married. "It's a bit difficult," I said. "I've got something on at 5 o'clock."

"What do you mean, you've got something on?" said Les. "Nothing ever happens here. If it does, I know about it. And I've organised this especially for you so that you can see my team."

"I'll get there as quickly as I can," I said.

Immediately the service was over, I rushed back to the island and caught the second half of the match. How romantic is that? Immediately after you get married, you rush off to a football match.

Les is very proud of the fact that he coached the Anguillan team. As he points out, it's something he has in common with the great Bobby Robson – two Fulham players who became international managers!

Before kick-off at Halifax Town.

Chapter 20

Showbiz XI – Final Curtain

Back in the murky mists of time every football team had two wingers. The advantage of being a winger was that you kept out of those goalmouth mêlées where people could get hurt and you got to take corner kicks where you got a free shot without anybody bothering you. The disadvantage was that you were the player closest to the crowd and the one who could hear all the abuse that was being hurled at you

Playing in a testimonial for Steve Perryman at White Hart Lane, I was getting plenty from the Spurs fans, mainly in connection with my allegiance to Fulham. Halfway through the first half the ball fell at my feet about thirty-five yards out and without looking up I thumped it in the direction of the opposite goal. When I looked up, I saw it sail into the back of the net. It certainly shut up the home fans and I chuckled to myself because I didn't know whether it was supposed to be a cross or a shot and to be honest it could have finished up anywhere in the ground.

Sometimes luck is on your side, and sometimes it isn't. Playing in a charity match at Birmingham City against Midlands heroes like Jasper Carrott and Trevor Francis, I chipped a ball over the opposing keeper. As it headed towards the goal, a musician in a band standing near the goalposts and waiting to play at half-time put down his sousaphone, ran on to the pitch and punched the ball over the bar, upon which the referee awarded a goal-kick. Lucky it wasn't a clarinet, or I'd have told him where to stick it.

By the 1980s the Showbiz XI had raised over £3 million for many deserving charities and, as well as still playing, I was made the team's honorary president. People often asked me who the best players were. In the early days Tommy Steele was good. Tommy kept himself really fit and was the same weight as in the days when he was a teenage rock 'n' roller. But probably the best player of all was Rod Stewart. On the books of Brentford as a junior player, he surely would have made the grade had he not discovered he was even better at singing. Rod played several times for the Showbiz XI and once before a match caused a sensation by landing on the centre circle in a helicopter.

Showbiz XI play to a full house at Huddersfield for the dependents of the Bradford City fire disaster. Line-up includes Frank Worthington, Tommy Cannon, Rick Wakeman, Jeremy Beadle, Lennie Bennett, Jess Conrad, singers Jim Diamond and Jim Dooley, Frazer Hines and stars of Emmerdale and Coronation Street.

After the Bradford City fire disaster in 1985 we were asked to take a team to Yorkshire to raise money for the dependents of the many people who perished in the fire. Obviously, we couldn't play the game in Bradford but Huddersfield Rugby League Club lent us their ground, and I put a team together that included Rick Wakeman, Jeremy Beadle, Tommy Cannon (from Cannon and Ball) and a number of actors including stars from *Emmerdale* and *Coronation Street*. Our opponents were the legendary stars of Leeds United – Jack Charlton, Peter Lorimer, Johnny Giles, etc. (I know, brave weren't we?) Although the fixture was hastily arranged without time to maximise publicity, when our coach arrived there were queues around the block.

We were in the dressing room getting changed when Frank Worthington walked in. "Other dressing room for the ex-pros," someone shouted.

"No, I'm playing for you," said Frank. "I've always wanted to be in show business."

Beadle's About – in the dressing room.

We ran out to a packed house. Clips from the game that night were shown on ITV's *News At Ten*. I don't remember the score. It doesn't matter. What does matter is that we were able to raise lots of money for those people who suffered as a result of one of football's biggest disasters.

I played my last game for the Showbiz XI in 1989. In a game at Maidstone I was kicked bang on the knee. It was very painful and Barry Fry, the Maidstone manager, carried me off the field and into the dressing room. As I lay on the bench, he put an ice pack on my knee and said, "Now try to bend it."

"What happens if I can't?" I asked.

"Then it's probably broken," said Barry. I did a quick mental check of all

Ouch! Barry Fry carries me off the pitch at Maidstone, my final game.

the jobs I had coming up over the next few weeks and how I was going to feel if I couldn't do them.

When I found I could bend my knee, Barry said, "Right, now get back out and run it off."

Dreena, who was at the game, said to me when we got home, "You're fifty now. Any injuries you get are going to take longer to clear up. Maybe this is the time to call it a day."

Since then my football has been restricted to kick-abouts with the kids in the garden. I think she was right. Women usually are.

Chapter 21

Dicks Out

Edward Burston had a dream. His dream, he told me, was that Fulham would be rid of Ernie Clay and of his plan to get wealthy at the expense of his club. In Clay's place would be a board of genuine Fulham supporters. He was a man who shunned publicity and his plan was that I, with my media profile, would be chairman and he, with his money, would be the power behind the scenes. Since we were such good friends I was sure we would work well together.

Sadly, before his dream could come true, Edward died in his early forties. After his death, all the things he feared came to fruition. In 1984 Ernie Clay bought the freehold of the ground from the Church Commissioners for £900,000. This was not very good business on behalf of the Church Commissioners because, not long after, Clay sold it to Marler Estates for almost £9 million, thus making a tidy profit for him and his family. Marler's plans were fairly obvious when in 1987 they bought Queen's Park Rangers' ground from Jim Gregory, and their chairman David Bulstrode announced his intention of merging Fulham with QPR, and playing at Loftus Road, leaving Craven Cottage free for redevelopment. Subsequently, Marler were taken over by Cabra Estates, but before they could continue their redevelopment plans Cabra, as luck would have it for Fulham fans, went bust. Throughout this time there were very great fears among us Fulhamites that our beloved Craven Cottage would be bulldozed to the ground and replaced by those luxury flats.

It was then that Bill Muddyman emerged, attempting to bring a period of stability to the club he supported while rectifying much of the mess he inherited. He brought with him a chairman who this time was a real Fulham man, Jimmy Hill. No-one doubted Jimmy's love of the club or his best intentions but little money was available, results were generally disappointing and the stadium became very run down. Many seats were missing in the Riverside Stand after vandals broke into the ground, and weeds were growing on the terraces. The Putney End was starting to look like an allotment. A vital letter was missing on the sign high up on the back of the Riverside Stand, the

The stars turn out for Jimmy Hill's Goaldiggers team at Tonbridge. Pictured amongst the girls are me (on left), Tom Courtenay, Jimmy, David Frost, Charlton's Derek Ufton, Richard O'Sullivan, George Cohen, Michael Crawford and John Hollins.

view seen by passengers on boats that sailed past the ground. ULHAM FOOTBALL CLUB, it said, contradicting the brilliantly named fanzine, *There's Only One F in Fulham*. In this case, there was no F in Fulham.

The choice of managers wasn't great. Alan Dicks, an old friend of Jimmy Hill, was brought in but that season Fulham avoided relegation to Division Four by just one place. The familiar cry rang round the terraces, "Dicks out!" And then, as the joke goes, we got Arthur Cox.

Some fans drifted away, attendances plummeted. Local MP David Mellor defected to Chelsea, where he joined his friend John Major. Later he was famously pictured with a young lady while wearing the Chelsea strip. Again the jokers had a field day. If he'd worn the Fulham strip, they said, he'd never have scored.

My pal Alex Shooter and I continued to go because whatever division we were in and no matter how the results went, we loved the Craven Cottage experience and we had this very strong feeling that it might not be there much longer and we should enjoy it while we could. Besides, where else would we go for our football? The lowest point came on November 15, 1991, when we were

Spot the spectator – Fulham v Bradford City, May 1992. As the weeds grow on the terraces, two lonely fans try to find something to be cheerful about.

beaten 2–0 at home by non-league Hayes in Round 1 of the FA Cup. We trudged away from the ground in the dark and cold saying, "It can't get worse than this."

In truth, there weren't many of us left, so few that it almost came down to announcing the crowd changes to the team. But it was a time when we grew very close to the players and often after a game we'd finish up having a few

This time Jimmy organises a tennis tournament. I'm there with some familiar faces including Graham Cole from The Bill, Eddie 'The Eagle' Edwards, Tessa Wyatt and Patti Boyd. Pop trivia: Patti had three hit songs written about her by two famous husbands – Wonderful Tonight and Layla by Eric Clapton and Something by George Harrison.

beers in Crocs in the Fulham Road with big Jim Stannard ("He's fat, he's round and he's worth a million pound") and Terry Hurlock. Terry was one of football's hard men, but off the pitch he was one of the nicest guys you could meet. Isn't that often the case? Sadly, Hurlock's career ended at Fulham when in a pre-season friendly – that word 'friendly' again – a Brentford defender launched himself at Terry, broke his leg and put him out of the game for ever. The hard man finally humbled.

Chapter 22

Celebrity Reporter

In 1991 the *Sunday Express* introduced a new feature on its sports pages: the celebrity report. Each week a celebrity would be despatched to some far-flung ground to report on a game featuring the team he, or sometimes she, supported. When I got the call from the paper's sports editor, Peter Watson, I was delighted to join the roster (shades of my days on *Soccer Star*) until I heard where the venue was: Hartlepool. Well, it was a ground I hadn't been to before, so that could be interesting.

The trip took almost an entire day. It would have been quicker to get to Majorca – and a darned sight warmer. The train journey involved changing at Darlington and Thornaby and when I got to Hartlepool I struggled to find a restaurant that was open for lunch, among all the boarded-up shops. The ground must have been the draughtiest in the country. With a yawning gap on one side the wind fairly whipped in off the North Sea. It was November and it was bleak.

Even bleaker was the game. The story of it was that we hardly had a shot on goal and we lost 2–nil. So the gist of my report centred around the remarkable fact that so many dedicated Fulham fans would spend so much of their hard-earned cash and give up an entire day of a precious weekend to watch something so uninspired. The journey home seemed twice as long.

In March 1993, the *Sunday Express* came calling again. After the round trip to Hartlepool, they took pity on me and offered me a home game against Reading. If there's one thing that's more difficult to write about than an abysmal 2–nil defeat, it's a nil–nil draw. Two celebrity reports done and still looking for a win.

September 1993. Another home game, this time v Bradford City. I'm looking for a new angle so the club say I can sit in the dugout alongside Ray Lewington. Ray is a joy to watch. Unlike some coaches and managers who are like bully boy sergeant-majors, he is a great encourager of players. "Nice ball, son," he'll shout. "Well played." All very positive. Don Mackay, the manager, is shouting advice, too, though I'm not sure they can decipher his Scottish accent.

SPORT

Farrell's finish brings light relief to dug-out

FOR MANY years Fulham was run by a comedian, Tommy Trinder based his act on the ineptitude of the team and the sparseness of the crowd.

Gags like: "There were so few people here last week someone shot a stag on the terraces" or "It's the only club where crowd changes are announced to the team."

Fulham had plenty of comedians on the pitch too — Tosh Chamberlain, Les Strong as well as Rodney Marsh and George Best, who are touring with their comedy double act. They could all play a bit, too.

These days there isn't so much to laugh about at Fulham as I discovered when I boldly went where no Sunday Express celebrity reporter has been before — into the dug-out.

A wise move after Kevin Keegan's experience? Maybe not. But Fulham is the friendly club of football. Until a bunch of hooligans from Cardiff hit town two weeks ago, nobody could recall any trouble at Craven Cottage — apart from one occasion when an old lady got on to the pitch and hit the referee over the head with an umbrella.

After 40 years of watching Fulham as a fan on the terraces, in the stand or even the direc-

CELEBRITY REPORT
by David Hamilton
Disc jockey and TV presenter
Fulham 1 Bradford 1

tors' box, being in the dug-out was the nearest I could get to being part of the action. I could hear the raw language, feel the crunching tackles. From my privileged seat the game seemed faster and more exciting.

Manager Don Mackay enjoyed himself. He spent most of the first half with a broad smile on his face while engaged

Man of the match
Gary Brazil (Fulham)

in a shouting contest to the players with his assistant, former Fulham favourite Ray Lewington.

I doubt whether they understood his Dundee accent or could hear his advice, but I did decipher "Get tight", "Slide it", "We've got to hit the front", and plenty of "Be patient".

When referee Allan Gunn wouldn't let the trainer on to treat an injured player, Don said: "The referee's indecision is final." The smile disappeared from Don's face when City's Sean McCarthy slotted home near the end of the first half.

Fulham lost winger Julian Hails with a hamstring injury and sent on Mark Cooper. With a squad of 17 and no reserves, injuries are critical to Mackay. How he must envy Kenny Dalglish, his successor at Blackburn, who just spent another £2.75m on Paul Warhurst.

In the 75th minute his smile returned and he was out to the touchline when Sean Farrell hammered in a 25-yard drive.

Don has put together a team that try to play good football. In Simon Morgan they have a captain in the Ray Lewington mould who always gives 100 per cent. What they need is ten more like him.

I have a feeling Fulham's style might be more successful in a higher division. With a small squad and a lack of firepower up front, people expect a long, hard winter at Craven Cottage. Some of Fulham's finishing had Don and Ray on their feet holding their heads in their hands.

Perhaps it's time to bring back the comedians.

Sponsored by

HIGH-FLIERS . . . Martin Pike and Tim Steele clash as Simon Morgan looks on

SUNDAY Express

Fulham take spot luck from a lottery

THIS is Houdini Hamilton reporting. Two down with nine minutes to go and Fulham, the club I have supported for 40 years, were sliding out of the FA Cup in a torrential downpour.

What drama. Two penalties in two minutes. Two magnificent spot-kicks by Micky Adams — and here we are heading back to Craven Cottage for a replay.

It is not often that Fulham break the box office record but they did it here in deepest Kent. 3,350 fans — ten times the average home gate — crammed into the tiny Homelands Ground to see the Beazer Homes League part-timers take on Fulham.

Covering the match marked a personal anniversary for me. Forty years ago, at the age of 16, I wrote a weekly column for

CELEBRITY REPORT
By David Hamilton
DJ and TV presenter
Ashford .... 2 Fulham 2

Raich Carter's Soccer Star. A lot has changed in the old game since then.

After what seemed like a week of continuous rain, it was a miracle this game was played at all. On a heavily sanded gluepot of a pitch, it looked as though the National Lottery had come to Ashford!

As Jimmy Hill said to me at half-time: "Football is a passing game and on this pitch it is impossible to pass."

Ashford played some neat football in the driving rain and Fulham's worst fears came true — courtesy of a 29-year-old gas-

fitter. Ashford striker Dave Arter, spotting one of those only too familiar holes in the Fulham defence, stormed into the gap and smashed the ball into the back of the net giving Jim Stannard no chance.

Fulham's best effort came at the start of the second half when a header from Rob Haworth hit the bar but, as they pressed forward, there was always the danger of being caught on the break.

Sure enough, Arter headed down and Nicky Dent hit the ball home.

Immediately afterwards, Dent, who had earlier been booked, could well have got a hat-trick with two splendid efforts which went close, one of them crashing against a post.

Halfway through the second half, the Hamilton sense of humour had totally deserted me. Just as it seemed Fulham would

MAN OF THE MATCH
Micky Adams (Fulham)

never score, Kevin Moore surged forward on a stirring run and was tripped in the penalty area. Adams netted from the spot.

Two minutes later, there was uproar when the referee awarded a second penalty for handball and the Ashford players chased him to the corner flag. After all the fuss, Adams scored his second penalty.

Sponsored by

ASHFORD scorers Dave Arter and Nicky Dent

Celebrity reporter in dugout with Ray Lew and Denis Signy from the Sunday Express.

When the referee fails to let the trainer on to treat an injured player, Don says, "The referee's indecision is final."

In the end, it's another draw 1-1.

For 1994 I'm given a cup game – away at Ashford Town from the Beazer Homes League, a banana skin if ever there was one. It was a game that should never have been played. It chucked it down with rain all day and the pitch was like a bog. Were it not for the fact that Sky were covering it, it surely would have been postponed and my celebrity column would not have appeared. As it was, the pitch was a great leveller. As Jimmy Hill said at half-time, it was impossible to pass the ball. With ten minutes to go, Fulham were two down and then, remarkably, in one of his first games as a referee, Andy D'Urso awarded Fulham two penalties in two minutes and Micky Adams scored from both. If you're ever rude about Andy again, remember how kind he was to us on that day.

So four games as a celebrity reporter, and not a win. How Fulhamish is that?

FULHAM
2000

Help Save Our Heritage

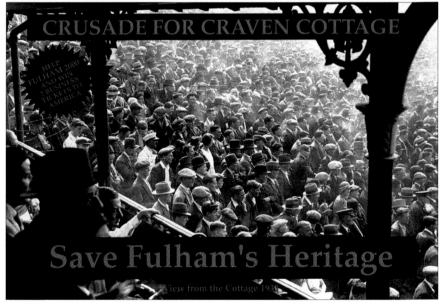

CRUSADE FOR CRAVEN COTTAGE

HELP
FULHAM 2000
AND WIN
2 BUSINESS
TICKETS TO
AMERICA

Save Fulham's Heritage

View from the Cottage 1939

Chapter 23

They Think It's All Over

For nearly twenty years after Ernie Clay became chairman the future of Fulham Football Club was in grave doubt. The club had moved to Craven Cottage in 1896 and it was very doubtful that the club would still be there to celebrate one hundred years on the site. In 1993 the ground was owned by the Royal Bank of Scotland. To buy it back the club would need to find £7.5 million, and that year a bunch of supporters founded Fulham 2000, a scheme whereby the fans themselves would attempt to raise the money by their own contributions and fundraising events. It was called the Crusade For Craven Cottage. Chairman of Fulham 2000 was Melvin Tenner, leader of the Supporters' Club. The treasurer was Geoff Faulkner and other members of the committee were Fulham chairman Jimmy Hill, vice-chairman Bill Muddyman, Richard Jones, Dominic Lang and Alan Williams, a member of the Vice-Presidents' Club who had their own lounge in the Riverside Stand. I was very honoured to be asked to be a patron along with Johnny Haynes and George Best and I set the ball rolling by writing out a cheque for £100 at a press launch at the club in March, 1994.

Supporters rallied round and hundreds of thousands of pounds were raised. Alan Williams was particularly active in organising events. An outstanding one was the FA Cup final anniversary dinner at the Heathrow Park Hotel on May 19, 1995. First came the re-match, which this time Fulham won, thanks to Peter Mellor keeping his legs closed. Alan planned the evening event meticulously. He asked me to be the compere, and the special guest on stage was Kenneth Wolstenholme, the man who uttered the immortal words, "They think it's all over... it is now," as England's last goal went in at the 1966 World Cup final. Alan invited Ken and me to lunch at his home in Ruislip the day before and over a splendid meal laid on by his wife, Beryl, went through the running order for the evening. On the night itself he was still giving me instructions as he dressed in his hotel room before dinner. Not surprisingly, it all ran like clockwork with Ken Wolstenholme recalling memories of the '75 final with Alec Stock.

Dinner in Majorca with (from left) Alex Shooter, a friend of the Swain family, Rita Swain, my daughter Jane, my son David, and Kim Shooter.

While all this good work was going on, the team was struggling on the pitch. In January 1996 only 2,196 people watched the home game against Scunthorpe and days later Fulham sank to its lowest ever position – 91st in the Football League – and was in grave danger of slipping into the Conference. By

Alec Stock is warmly welcomed by Ken Wolstenholme at Fulham's cup final anniversary dinner.

this time the club was surviving purely thanks to the generosity of its supporters. Director Cyril Swain, a lovely man with a delightful family, bought full-back Robbie Herrera from Queen's Park Rangers with £40,000 of his own money, a gift he very much played down at the time. It was a gesture that typified the spirit behind Fulham 2000 and there's no doubt that, were it not for the efforts of all the people who supported it, it would indeed have been all over at Craven Cottage.

From the picture album

My favourite shot of me and David junior.

Party time with my son and daughter and Debbie and Tony Blackburn.

Chapter 24

The Man on the Mike

In December, 1996, I was asked if I would like to take over hosting the half-time entertainment at Fulham. My first match was against Leyton Orient on December 14 and we drew 1–1. The half-time entertainment began with the Fulham Flutter where the winner whose draw ticket was picked out of a drum would come on to the pitch and collect a cash prize. The draw was usually done by a celebrity, an ex-Fulham player or even a current player who was injured. There would be the reading of the half-time scores and then a penalty shoot-out between two teams of schoolchildren. This would take place in both goal areas and I soon discovered that the smaller and younger the kids were, the more the crowd enjoyed it.

By the end of my first (half) season, I was MC-ing a promotion celebration, Fulham's first in thirteen years. Under Micky Adams, in his first managerial job, Fulham had been promoted with four games in hand. On April 12, 1997, eleven and a half thousand, our biggest crowd of the season, came along to see Northampton beat us 1–nil. "They're spoiling the party," I said to Micky, who just grunted.

So the champagne was put on ice. But we made no mistake in the final home match against Hull City. Simon Morgan scored twice, Hull had no reply and Micky and the boys did a lap of honour after the match. Out on the pitch, with the microphone in my hand, I could sense the feelgood factor enveloping the ground. That feelgood factor of a promotion season runs right through a football club and affects every department, not just the players – the management, the corporate people, everybody.

During the close season I was asked if, as well as the half-time entertainment, I'd also like to take over the announcing duties for the coming season. Up to this time the announcer had been in a box on the corner of the Cottage balcony. Both box and balcony were falling apart – today they'd be regarded as a health hazard – and the box also provided a dreadful view of the game. It was so far away from the Hammersmith End that, if a goal was scored there, it was very difficult to say who scored it, so after a while it was agreed

Mohamed Al Fayed arrives at Craven Cottage.

that my vantage point would be a spare dugout among those reserved for disabled people in front of the Riverside Stand. It was also decided that my friend Alex Shooter would play the music (from a box high in the Riverside) and then join me in the dugout to help confirm who the goalscorers were. While all this was being discussed in the summer, little did I know that the 'white knight' Fulham had dreamed of for so long was about to come riding in.

I first met Mohamed Al Fayed on the pitch at Craven Cottage before the opening match of the 1997–98 season against Wrexham. I shook his hand on three separate occasions. There were two reasons for that. Photographers were buzzing around and, to be honest, I was not one to miss a photo opportunity. Secondly, I was genuinely pleased to see him. He gave me a quizzical look, as if to say, "Who is this guy who keeps shaking my hand?" The team didn't let him down. For his first match a first-half goal by Mike Conroy was enough to beat the visitors 1–nil.

Mr Al Fayed made the club a pledge. He would see Fulham in the Premiership in five years. In line with his ambitious plans, he brought in a high profile team – Kevin Keegan as chief operating officer and Ray Wilkins as manager. Within no time they had acquired Fulham's first £1 million signing, Paul Peschisolido, and not long afterwards Chris Coleman joined from Blackburn and became one of the finest centre-backs in the history of the club. On the balcony

The chairman surveys the Riverside Stand before kick-off.

of the Cottage Kevin Keegan introduced me to another new player with the words, "This boy will have a tremendous future at the club." The boy with the dreadlocks announced himself: "Rufus Emmanuel Brevett." He wouldn't be the biggest full-back we'd ever had, but what a brave, tough, lion-hearted player he turned out to be.

I must say I liked Keegan. Not only was he a great motivator of players but his PR was good. He always seemed to have time for people at the club and had a very likeable personality.

Fulham's training ground was in Roehampton and one day when walking my dog in Richmond Park I was enormously impressed to see Keegan leading the team on a pre-season run round the park. It was quite a while since he'd played yet there he was out in front on a seven-mile circuit of the park, leading by example. Fulham finished 1997–98 sixth, a pretty good position for a team promoted the previous season. During the summer another offer to expand my duties at Craven Cottage came along when I was asked to host a post-match question-and-answer session with George Cohen in one of the club's lounges, so now I was doing three jobs. George, as I swiftly discovered, reads the game better than anybody. How lucky we are at Fulham that one of our greatest players (459 games for Fulham, his only club, and 37 caps for England) should have been a member of the only England team to win the World Cup.

Kevin Keegan enjoying success.

Rufus Emmanuel Brevett

By 1998–99 Kevin Keegan was in sole charge. Maik Taylor became the regular first team goalkeeper, an ex-Army man and solid as a rock. Keegan's old colleagues, Paul Bracewell and Peter Beardsley, brought some experience to the team. Inspired signings were Steve Finnan and Geoff Horsfield, a real old fashioned battering-ram of a centre-forward. Pudsey, the kit man, was a bit of a comedian, and told me how Geoff got his nickname, 'The Horse'. "He has the speed of a racehorse, the strength of a carthorse and the brains of a rocking horse." I'm sure it was an affectionate gag because everybody liked The Horse and the crowd certainly took him to their hearts – a player who would always be welcome back at Craven Cottage.

Kit Symonds joined his Welsh international colleague Chris Coleman. Not many forwards got past Chris, and he and Kit were more than just a defensive partnership. Kit scored a remarkable number of goals for a defender, 12 league goals in that season alone. I can see him now rising over the opposing defence

to head one in. Fulham walked the Division Two league title with 101 points, and for the second time in two seasons I was out there on the pitch MC-ing a promotion celebration. How nice for Simon Morgan to be part of it. Having been there through the lean years, he was now almost the only remaining member of the Micky Adams promotion side of two years before. Just one more promotion was needed now to fulfil Mohamed Al Fayed's pledge. Surely nothing could spoil the party this time?

But it did. Kevin Keegan resigned, to take up the job as England manager. The Fulham faithful were up in arms about his disloyalty to the club but to manage your country's international team is probably every coach's dream and Kevin couldn't resist the challenge. He would be the first of several Fulham managers to realise that the grass isn't always greener on the other side.

Under Mohamed Al Fayed's chairmanship, things were moving fast. Enormous improvements were being made to the stadium, and a new training ground was acquired at Motspur Park, which housed the club's offices as well as training

Geoff Horsfield and Kit Symonds.

facilities for the players. With Kevin Keegan gone, Paul Bracewell relinquished his playing duties and took over as manager until the next big name came along.

Simon Morgan was awarded a testimonial, deservedly after all he'd been through with the club. He'd been Fulham's player of the decade. Signed from Leicester in 1990, he was thought to be injury prone, but that didn't stop him playing 400 games for the Whites. He was a good player in what was at one time a poor team, but got his reward when he was part of two promotion teams towards the end of the decade. I was on his testimonial committee with David Gardner, Paul Kenny from GMB – the union that for several seasons were Fulham's sponsors – Anna Monk and Bob Howes.

We launched the fund with a reception at the RAC Club in Pall Mall, where I handed Simon a cheque for £500 from Crocs Restaurant in Fulham Road (now The Coalition) kindly donated by its owner, Brian Mason, one of the few people to be a season ticket holder at both Fulham and Chelsea. Simon was an enormously popular player at Fulham, once again because the supporters knew he always gave 100 per cent but also because he was there through the good times and the bad. He epitomised the expression 'a good pro'. More than that, Simon had a good sense of humour and turned out to have a decent writing style, as witnessed in his book *On Song for Promotion*. I believe his will

probably be the last testimonial we will ever see at Fulham. Players don't stay at clubs for long these days – the era of the one-club man like Johnny Haynes and George Cohen has gone – and players now earn so much more than the fans in the stands. The testimonial was the reward to loyal club servants and a bonus to those who hadn't earned a fortune in what is a short career. As we entered the new millennium, the game was changing beyond recognition, and Simon Morgan represented the last of the old regime. Thanks to the generosity of the supporters, Simon's testimonial fund raised £120,000. He deserved it.

Jean Tigana was appointed manager for the 2001–02 season. Not many of us got to know him well. He spent much of the time on the touchline sucking a toothpick, but what a start he got off to. Fulham began the season

Simon Morgan celebrates.

Jean Tigana

with 11 consecutive wins. Many of the goals were scored by Louis Saha and Barry Hayles, several others by Luis Boa Morte. It was the most stunning start to a season we had ever known. By the end of the year Fulham had lost only one game. Early on we were in no doubt that we were going to be promoted, and this was the big one – to the Premiership. In the end, we walked it with 101 points, the same tally as Kevin Keegan's promotion season, but with even more goals: 90 instead of 79.

Simon Morgan played only one game that season. Against Wolverhampton Wanderers on April 24 he came on as a substitute for about 13 minutes. During that time he barely touched the ball but when I announced his name as 'Man of the Match' there was a mighty roar from the crowd. Simon saw the funny side of it, but he knew the supporters were showing their appreciation for everything he'd done for the club. There was a carnival atmosphere that day. Four days later at our final home game against Wimbledon I was MC-ing a promotion celebration for the third time. Mohamed Al Fayed's pledge had come true. He promised we'd be in the Premiership within five years and we'd done it in four.

The only thing that marred that wonderful promotion season was the road accident that finished Chris Coleman's career shortly after the turn of the year. Chris's car came off the road near his home in Surrey. When the fire crew finally located him, Chris was trapped in the car and at one time the firemen feared they might have to amputate his foot to cut him free. In the end, they

didn't have to do that but Chris's injuries were so bad that he was never able to play for Fulham again although Mark Hughes did put him on as a substitute in the last minute of an international for Wales. Who says there's no sentiment in football?

Fulham's first season in the Premiership began at, of all places, Old Trafford. The team played brilliantly against Manchester United with two goals from

Barry Hayles, always in the thick of the action.

A typical goal from the superb Louis Saha, this one during our exile at Loftus Road.

Louis Saha – no wonder United later poached him – before finally succumbing 3–2. During the summer Tigana had signed some sublimely talented players like Steed Malbranque ('Steeeeed' as the crowd liked to call him) and Sylvain Legwinski, and paid a club record £7 million for goalkeeper Edwin van der Sar. The record didn't last long when a month later he paid over £11 million for Steve Marlet. This was his one bad signing. Marlet failed to deliver and was a great disappointment to the crowd.

Chris Coleman and Steed Malbranque.

After Fulham's first season in the Premiership, they had to vacate Craven Cottage because terracing was not allowed in the top league. It was decided the club would ground-share with Queen's Park Rangers and, though the people at QPR were very welcoming, this came as quite a culture shock to the Fulham faithful. The council flats of Shepherd's Bush were a stark contrast to the £1–£2 million Victorian and Edwardian houses of SW6, not to mention the listed buildings and the river. In fairness to the Loftus Road ground, it did have a good atmosphere, especially with the spectators being so close to the pitch. (The cover of Stan Bowles' autobiography showed him standing by a goalpost waiting for a

corner kick to come over, reading a copy of the *Sporting Life* that he'd borrowed from someone behind the goal.) But for each and every one of us Fulhamites, ground-sharing was like being a fish out of water. Many feared that having left Craven Cottage, we might never go back.

As the 'man on the mike' at Fulham, my problem was that there had never been a really good vantage point to work from, one that had a clear view of the game with proximity to the fourth official for information of upcoming substitutions – a triple substitution, which could happen from time to time, was particularly difficult. That is why I always liked to have a helper with me, a second pair of eyes or even legs if necessary, to run across to one of the benches where players or staff from either side were only too happy to confirm who scored a goal. (Apart from the odd joker who thought it was fun to give me the wrong information!)

My pal Alex Shooter had long ago moved off to a seat in the stand and with his departure I was no longer responsible for the choice of music. I know that a lot of people thought that as I was a radio DJ, I picked the music but in fact I hadn't done so for quite a while. At QPR I didn't need a helper. My vantage point was excellent. Either at the entrance to the players' tunnel or at the end of the substitutes' bench, I could see every bit of play and as I was right behind the fourth official, I had a perfect view of every substitute coming on or off.

The team did pretty well in their two seasons at QPR, finishing 14th and then 9th under Chris Coleman. I compered Fulham's end of season dinner, as I usually did, at the Novotel, Hammersmith, and signed off the evening saying, "See you in August back at the Cottage." Everybody was relieved that we'd survived the two years at QPR and now we were going home. Under the guidance of Fulham director Mark Collins, the work that had gone on for the last two years had turned Fulham into a stadium fit for the Premier League with seats all round and for the first time a covered stand at the Putney End, new yet in keeping with the listed buildings.

A summer break and then we'd be back and I'd be there again as Fulham's 'man on the mike'. Or so I thought.

Chapter 25

Sacked

A few days after the end of season dinner in May 2004, the phone rang at my home in Barnes. At the other end of the line was Emma Taylor, from Fulham's marketing department. "Just to let you know," she said. "We won't be needing your services next season."

"Really?" I said, trying desperately not to sound shocked. "Why is that?"

She went into some explanation that Fulham was far too friendly a place, that they wanted to turn it into Fortress Fulham and they wanted someone who would whip the crowd into a frenzy.

There were a lot of things I could have said. I could have said that most clubs would envy a crowd as well behaved as ours. The only trouble I ever witnessed over the years was when Cardiff City came to the Cottage and some of their followers in the Putney End threatened our people in the Stevenage Road Stand, forcing the players to leave the pitch for ten minutes. We had a record of exemplary behaviour that would have been hard to equal in any league. As for whipping the crowd up, I could have mentioned that I'd had no complaints from The Beatles or The Rolling Stones when I compered their concerts or, indeed, from the likes of David Cassidy, The Bay City Rollers or Leo Sayer. Instead, I just said, "I wish you well."

"We'd like to thank you for all you've done," she said, "and offer you a ticket for next season."

I thought about that for a moment, and then pondered how I would feel sitting in the crowd on my own. "That's very kind of you," I said. "But I don't really want to go on my own. Is it possible to have two?" I could have added that if I ever invited her to one of my shows, I wouldn't expect her to come on her own.

"I'll look into that," she said, "and come back to you."

So that was it. Sacked from the job I loved. It seemed tough. I hadn't made any mistakes. Week after week all the information I imparted was correct – goalscorers, substitutes, half-time scores – the transition to QPR had worked smoothly and I'd been there through a period of great success: three promotions and three years in the Premiership. Now, amid all the euphoria of going home to the Cottage, I was out with the washing.

The weeks of summer drifted by and several potential successors were tried out in pre-season friendlies. Friends and fellow-supporters rang and asked where I was and reported that the people doing my job were awful. I had to explain to them what had happened. A few days before the first home match one season ticket arrived with a letter from Emma Taylor, stating that the directors had rejected my request for a second one but the seat next to mine was available if I wanted to buy it for the season. I thought about it very carefully and eventually decided that I would buy it for my son, David.

Meanwhile, the press got wind of my sacking and Fulham supporter Dave Kidd started a campaign in *The Sun* newspaper demanding that I should be reinstated. He called it Diddygate, and when *The Sun* published a Diddygate poll on the day of Fulham's first match of the season, away at Man City, an overwhelming majority of readers voted for me to come back. Ignoring the outcome of the poll, a club spokesperson said the decision would stand, blaming it on manager Chris Coleman, though he later denied this.

So I missed out on the glorious day when Fulham returned home to Craven Cottage on August 21, 2004. But at least I didn't have to sit on my own. My son was away, but luckily my friend David Roodyn had a spare ticket and I sat with him high up in the Riverside Stand. David had written a very nice article about me in the club's programme. Reading it was a bit like reading my obituary. Unsurprisingly for an August day, the sun was shining, once again there was a carnival atmosphere and the visitors were Bolton Wanderers. Out on the pitch was my successor, a stand-up comedian called Dominic Frisbee. He generously thanked me for my work at Fulham and mentioned my encyclopaedic knowledge of the club. There was a warm round of applause from the Hammersmith End. Unfortunately, football supporters are not keen on gags. They have a quirky sense of humour, but what works in a comedy club doesn't necessarily go down well on a football pitch, and a joke about women voting that Moritz Volz had the best tackle in the Premiership fell as flat as a pancake. Worse was to follow and, in fairness to Dominic, not all was his fault. The DJ played a record with the f-word in it, the chairman's suit was splashed by the sprinkler on the pitch, and Keith Allen got in on the act introducing a bunch of men in tights calling themselves 'The Gayvenettes', a parody of The Cravenettes, a troupe of dancing girls the chairman had brought in some years previously. David Roodyn and I watched with horror as the scene unfolded in front of us. He turned to me and said, "It's the biggest disaster since Gallipoli." Snatches of it were shown on *Match Of The Day* and on Monday morning the newspapers splashed more stories about it.

On Monday morning, around 11 o'clock, I was in the middle of my radio show in London when I checked my mobile phone. There was a message from Mark Collins, the Fulham director, asking me to call him. When I called Mark back, he asked if I could come to a meeting with Mohamed Al Fayed at his office in Harrods that afternoon. "Can you tell me what it's about?" I asked.

"He wants to discuss the way ahead," said Mark. We arranged a time of 3 o'clock and Mark suggested I meet him first at his office where he ran Harrods Estates. As I put the phone down, I didn't want to assume too much, but I felt there was a chance that I was going to get my job back.

Making sure I wasn't late, I arrived at Mark's office just before three and, as we walked across Brompton Road to the Harrods building, Mark gave me little hint of the meeting to come. We took the escalator up several floors and walked into the boardroom, waiting for the great man to arrive.

After a couple of minutes he walked in with a flourish and plonked on the desk a bottle of whisky from his own distillery in Scotland and a ceramic phial full of Viagra pills. "These are what you need," he said, and at that moment I just had the feeling that the meeting was going to go well, so I told him a joke about some new pills that are a mixture of Viagra and Prozac: "If you don't get a f---, you don't give a f---." He roared with laughter, and I think it was then that he decided I was a comedian. Suddenly, his face turned serious. "So what's happened to you?" he asked. Until he said that, I'd assumed he knew all about my sacking and perhaps had even condoned it.

I explained about the letter from Emma Taylor and the board's rejection of a second ticket. "We weren't even asked," said Mark. Recovering from the shock of that, I then told him that I had bought a season ticket for the seat next to mine. "How much did you pay for it?" asked the chairman.

"Six hundred pounds," I replied. With that he reached into his breast pocket, handed me a wad of notes and left the room. "Where's he gone?" I asked Mark, thinking perhaps that was the end of the meeting. "He's gone to get some more money," he said.

While he was out of the room, I counted the money under the boardroom desk. It was four hundred and fifty pounds. A couple of minutes later he returned with another hundred and fifty.

During the time I was waiting, a line had come into my head that I just couldn't resist. "I don't think I should take cash from you with a name like Hamilton," I said, with an obvious reference to Neil Hamilton and the 'cash for questions' issue. Again he roared with laughter. "Why am I employing someone called Hamilton?" he said. "You're not," I said. "I've been sacked."

With that he said, "I want you back for the game tomorrow night. How much are we paying you?" I told him and he said, "No, we're not," and promptly gave me a considerable rise. "This is your job as long as you want to do it," he said. "And if you ever have trouble again, let me know. What I want you to do is tell the crowd I want to see the ground full every week. Can you do that?"

"I certainly can," I said.

He shook hands. "Then I'll see you tomorrow night."

There are good days and there are bad days. This was definitely a good day, and I didn't need the escalator to take me back to the ground floor. I could have flown there on my own.

Chapter 26

Back in Business

The following night I was back in business for the match against Middlesbrough. On the pitch at half-time, I quoted the words of Mark Twain: "Rumours of my death have been exaggerated." To a big cheer, I thanked the supporters who had voted for me in the *Sun* poll and thanked the chairman for giving me my job back. I also told the crowd that I was getting the blame for them being too quiet. "So make a lot of noise, or I'll get sacked again." (I don't think anyone these days says the Fulham crowd is quiet.)

Later I introduced my wife, Dreena, to Mohamed Al Fayed on the steps of the Riverside Stand. "This is Lady Hamilton," I said jokingly.

"I thought he was gay," said the chairman.

"Oh no," said Mrs H. "And the Viagra does work."

The night after the match Dreena and I were having dinner in a Thai restaurant in Barnes when who should walk in but the club's managing director, Jim Hone, and his wife. They sat a couple of tables away and when Jim spotted me, he walked over and said, "Come and join us for a drink when you've finished your meal."

"This should be interesting," I said to Mrs H.

After dinner we strolled over to their table and over a glass of champagne Jim said, "I'd like you to know that I had nothing to do with your sacking."

"Nobody did, Jim," I said. "I got sacked, but nobody did it."

"Oh, yes they did," said Jim, and proceeded to run off a couple of names of people who, for reasons best known to themselves, had decided they were going to get shot of me. They had loaded the bullets, and left Emma Taylor to fire the gun.

Once I was back it was agreed that the best place for me to be during the game was in the fourth official's dugout – in between the home and away dugouts – which I would share with the fourth official and representatives from the BBC and Sky. Gary Chivers, the ex-Chelsea player, was often in there, too. Because of the proximity to the Fulham bench, a lot of people thought he was on the coaching staff but, in fact, he was there working for Trans World

On the touchline with Alan Blackmore (right) who looks after the mascots and Simon Kew, who looked after me!

International. Also with us was my new helper, Simon Kew, whose brother Kevin was a regular in the disabled section of the ground along with their father, Del, and Del's girlfriend, Avril. Simon turned out to be brilliant to work with and we became a good team, having lots of laughs along the way with Gary. After a while, when the club brought in exercise bikes on the touchline, our dugout shrank until it became not much bigger than a telephone box. We all certainly became closer then!

Being in the dugout, we were close enough to the action on the pitch to feel the tackles as they went in and to hear the industrial language. But we didn't always have the best view in the world. With three or four coaches on the slope in front of us, we had to duck and dive sideways to see who scored a goal, but usually one of us was in the correct place to call it right. Basically, the media guys, Simon and I all helped each other out. Sometimes we had a monitor in there on which we could see action replays of goals, but after a while this practice was stopped because it was too easy for coaches to see things on the monitor and then harass the fourth official.

We became fascinated by the conduct of away managers. Some were out-and-out bully boys, and once Gary had a verbal spat with Ian Dowie, no doubt a hark back to an old rivalry on the pitch. We decided that Stuart Pearce of Manchester City was our favourite visiting manager. He gave one of his players an absolute bollocking and then sheepishly walked over to me and said, "I've tried being nice but it doesn't work."

Harry Redknapp always shook hands with me and had time for a chat; so did Pat Rice of Arsenal, Sammy Lee of Liverpool and Alan Curbishley when he was at Charlton. Before Man City's game at the Cottage in 2011 Brian Kidd, their assistant manager, came over to the dugout for a 20-minute chat before the match – a truly nice guy.

Being in the dugout I saw at first hand how much help the fourth official is able to be to the referee and how useful it is for the ref to be assisted by another pair of eyes operating from a different angle. It makes me wonder how they managed in the days before both referee and fourth official had an earpiece so they could speak to each other throughout the game. I'm not sure any ref particularly relishes being fourth official but Lee Probert was always a great laugh, livening up a cold afternoon in the dugout, and it was interesting to talk to Mark Halsey and hear about his battle with throat cancer and how he got back to doing the job he loves.

Referees are an easy target for criticism but they have only one chance to view an incident, unlike the pundits who can see it played back two or three times. Having watched them at close range, I think they do a pretty good job and when you see the referees from other countries you realise that ours are still probably the best in the world.

Chris Coleman remained in charge in our first season back at our ancestral home. One of the stars of the season was an American striker who would become one of those players the crowd really took to their hearts, who went in where it hurt and scored spectacular goals – Brian McBride. As I discovered, a nicer man you couldn't wish to meet. When I introduced him to George Cohen, telling him that George was part of the England team that won the World Cup, Brian's word was 'awesome'. He had a lovely wife and children. He loved Fulham and Fulham loved him, so much so that a bar in the Riverside Stand now bears his name, McBride's.

We finished the season better than we began it, with a 6–nil win over Norwich, which condemned them to relegation to the Championship. Their supporters were fantastic, never stopped singing and even stayed behind while our players came out with their families and waved to the crowd. On the mike I wished them well and said we looked forward to seeing them back at Craven Cottage in the future. Seven years later my wish for them came true.

Fulham finished 13th in the Premiership and the following season went one better. Showboating Jimmy Bullard arrived at the start of 2005–06 and it was clear from the word go that he wanted to take every free-kick and corner and cover every blade of grass on the pitch. The crowd loved him but up at Newcastle he suffered a terrible knee injury and from then on the team started to struggle. The result was the departure of Chris Coleman and the arrival of Lawrie Sanchez. Unfortunately, the long ball game he liked found little favour with the crowd, most of whom warmed to him no more than to his style of play. Mercifully, his time in charge was short.

Danny Murphy, Roy Hodgson and Brian McBride.

Roy Hodgson arrived just after Christmas 2007, a brilliant appointment – the most 'Fulhamish' manager since Alec Stock. In fact, the two had quite a lot in common: both 'gentleman' managers who liked their teams to play fairly and cleanly, both loved the passing game and both were advocates of 'pure' football. Hodgson came with a point to prove. Though he'd had great success abroad, he had yet to manage successfully at the highest level in England. The first part of 2008 was difficult, mainly because the team had struggled to win away from home for ages. On April 28, 2–nil down at half-time at Manchester City, we were dead and buried, and doomed to relegation, with two games still to go. Miraculously, with two great goals from Diomansy Kamara in the last 20 minutes and a penalty from Danny Murphy, we were still in with an outside chance of avoiding the drop. We needed to win our last two matches, and for other results to go our way as well.

We won our last home game against Birmingham, and so it was to Fratton Park for the final fixture of the season. With 15 minutes to go, we were drawing

Headmaster and author Peter Thomson and Alan Mullery pay tribute to our star central defender.

0–0 and down. Then suddenly, as if in slow motion, Danny Murphy rose like a phoenix in the penalty area to head the ball home. A header from Danny Murphy – how incredible is that? Reading lost, they went down and we stayed up on goal difference.

They called it The Great Escape, and it probably was the most remarkable escape from relegation the Premier League had ever known. Fulham won 4 of their last 5 games, 3 of them away. Roy 'Merlin' Hodgson had cast his magic spell. But, hey, we mustn't ever cut it that fine again. Too tough on the old ticker!

Season 2008–09 started with an away game at Hull. I had some friends in the city, was doing some work for the local radio station and wanted to go because it was a special occasion. Hull was the only city in Europe never to have a team in the top division, and now they'd made it at last. Fulham started well but in the end we were beaten by the occasion. Hull's crowd were urging them on, it was a day they would never forget and they just had to win a match that would go down in the city's history.

Hodgson had made some brilliant signings – the Australian goalkeeper Mark Schwarzer, striker Andy Johnson and tall central defender Brede Hangeland. After matches, in our question-and-answer session in the George Cohen Lounge, George raved about Brede. George is his biggest fan and pointed out how brilliant Brede is with the ball at his feet and how good his distribution is. He also remarked how much Bobby Zamora's game had improved under Roy Hodgson. In fact, so many of the players – Danny Murphy, Chris Baird and Simon Davies, to mention only three – upped their game under Roy. It's clear they liked him and liked playing for him.

On a personal note, in March 2009, *Match Of The Day 2* booked me for a feature on the Fulham–Manchester United game. Comedian Kevin Day did the feature and they filmed me in the dugout. As luck would have it, Fulham won 2–nil with goals from Danny Murphy and Zoltan Gera, and *MOTD 2* splashed it big. The season ended with Fulham in 7th place, our highest ever position in the top division, meaning that next year we'd be in Europe. We lost our final match against Everton 2–nil, but that didn't stop the celebrations. Cue the music, cue the players – out they came on their lap of honour.

Not only did we have our highest ever place, we also won the Fair Play award and Behaviour of the Public award. As Ian Dury would say, many reasons to be cheerful in SW6.

Chapter 27

Europe

O ur European adventure began with the visit of the Lithuanian team FK Vetra on August 6, 2009. None of us in the ground could have dreamed where it would lead by the following spring. Before the match I asked the crowd to join in a minute's silence for Sir Bobby Robson, who had died a few days previously at the age of 76. As always at the Cottage, the silence was impeccably observed. I know sometimes now it's customary for supporters to break into spontaneous applause but in this case the silence gave me the opportunity to reflect on that day long ago when I saw a young Bobby walking through Bishops Park after a morning's training, how I was once lucky enough to share a dinner table with him and his wife Elsie, along with George and Daphne Cohen and Johnny and Avril Haynes and how he had gone on to be a unique national treasure, adored and respected on every ground he went to. Of how many football people can we say that? A Fulham man of whom we can be justly proud.

Bobby brought us luck on the night, and Vetra were duly despatched. Amkar Perm were next up, and it was clear to me that players from eastern Europe and beyond were bound to cause pronunciation problems for any man on the mike. Luckily, EUFA insisted that announcements be made in both languages for the benefit of visiting fans and provided a translator for just that purpose. At the Amkar Perm game Simon, my right hand man, and I were very taken with the Russian lady charged with that role, to the point that I asked her if as well as reading out announcements about no smoking and respect for referees, she would also read out the Amkar team. Luckily, she jumped at my offer. I still had to do substitutes and goalscorers during the game, but what a relief not to have to read out eighteen Russian names all together!

As I got to know Roy Hodgson better, I realised what a decent and likeable man he is. Emails to him at the training ground were returned with a personal note shortly after morning training had finished. His handling of the media was brilliant. Though he was as capable as any manager of being heated on the touchline, he had cooled down enough to be measured and generous to the

officials and opposition in post-match interviews. His knowledge of football in Europe was considerable and by the time we had taken our first major scalp, that of the mighty Roma, in October, people were starting to take our European journey seriously. We then disposed of the holders, Shakhtar Donetsk, a 25-yard screamer from Bobby Zamora winning the tie for us.

March 18, 2010, was one of the most incredible nights in Fulham's history. Juventus had beaten us 3–1 in the first leg and when they scored in the second minute of the second leg at Craven Cottage, I sensed this was the night everything was going to go wrong. We now needed to score four goals,

Clint Dempsey

seemingly an impossible task against a club as big as Juventus. Bobby Zamora got the equaliser after nine minutes, Zoltan Gera got a brace, one before and one (a coolly taken penalty) after half-time, and people were now starting to believe this could be our year. The Fulham crowd, once accused of being so quiet and reserved, was now willing the team on, urging them to new heights. When Clint Dempsey scored our fourth goal in the 82nd minute, I'd never seen or heard an atmosphere like it at Craven Cottage.

At the end of the game I looked over from the dugout towards the Hammersmith End with tears in my eyes. I never thought

This painting by renowned artist Jason Bowyer – a staunch Fulham fan – is entitled "Stand up if you believe" and celebrates that great night against Juventus at the Cottage.

Fulham on their European journey. Standing: Bobby Zamora, Mark Schwarzer, Brede Hangeland, Stephen Kelly, Dickson Etuhu, Zoltan Gera; front: Simon Davies, Aaron Hughes, Damien Duff, Paul Konchesky, Chris Baird.

the team I had followed and supported for over sixty years would have a night like this. In a nail-biting finish, Fulham had beaten Juventus, one of the world's greatest football clubs, 4–1. In the quarter-final we were drawn at home to Wolfsburg, and Bobby Zamora and Damien Duff got the goals in our 2–1 win. Away at Wolfsburg a goal in the very first minute from Zamora – that man again – was enough to take us to the semis. This time our first leg was away to another German team, Hamburg, who had every incentive in the world since the final was due to be played on their ground. A Europa League final on your own ground was a mouth-watering prospect for any club. A crowd of 49,000 saw us draw 0–0 in the first leg at the Nordbank Arena, and on April 29 it was back to the Cottage for another memorable evening.

For me, and my role at the club, it was memorable for the wrong reasons. An hour and a half before kick-off I always test the microphone to make sure it's working. This evening not a word I was saying was coming out over the loudspeakers. I located a friendly steward in the stand who contacted one of the maintenance men. After checking the batteries in the mike and making sure it was faded up in the DJ box, he then set off in search of where any other trouble might be. Time was moving on, kick-off was ever nearer and I hadn't been able to do any of the announcements that EUFA required. With ten minutes to go, I finally legged it up to the security room at the back of the Riverside Stand. Though everybody was very friendly and welcoming, the microphone quality was poor at the time, and anything I had to say was so muffled that at half-time instructions came through not to say any more. Thus, on probably the greatest ever night at Craven Cottage, I was not able to announce to the jubilant crowd that Simon Davies had scored in the 69th minute and that seven minutes later Zoltan Gera had bagged the goal that would take us to the Europa League Cup final. Nor was I able to be a part of the celebrations at the end. Having abandoned the security box in the second half, I stood near the touchline at the end, speechless for once in my life.

I never really found out what caused Fulham's microphone not to function on the club's biggest night, but things brightened up when the invitation came from EUFA to take part in the coverage of the final in Hamburg. The idea was that my counterpart from Atletico Madrid and I would be part of the announcing team and would both be involved in warming up the crowd before the match. Before that there was a job to do for Channel 5 who were covering the final, and on May 5, before the game against Stoke City, I dropped in to the Sunset and Vine studio in Fulham Palace Road to record a long poem urging Fulham on to victory. The poem was to be used in the pre-match build-up on TV.

On the morning of May 11 I flew out with the team from Gatwick Airport en route to the club's biggest ever game. In the lounge at Gatwick I bumped into Archie Rhind-Tutt and his father, Simon. Archie is one of the new generation of Fulham fans. Fresh out of Charterhouse, he is starting to carve out a career in broadcasting and now writes a regular column in the excellent fanzine. Before matches I frequently give him a spare team sheet in exchange for his knowledge of some of the players' more unpronounceable names. I shall watch his progress with interest.

On board the plane the players and Roy Hodgson, Mike Kelly and Ray Lewington, together with the club's directors, were at the front. Supporters and members of the press were at the back. When we landed at Hamburg, I caught a quick and jovial conversation with directors Mark Collins and Michael Cole before a taxi whisked me off to the Nordbank Arena for an afternoon meeting. EUFA, as I discovered, leave little to chance and the following morning I was required for rehearsals at 10.30. I've done plenty of rehearsals in my life but never for a football match but, hey, there's a first time for everything.

The night before the match I was booked into the Steigenberger Hotel in Hamburg and that evening the club took several of the club's sponsors and supporters out to dinner at an excellent restaurant in the city. Each table was hosted by a member of the Fulham staff and the guests included staunch supporters who'd followed Fulham around Europe, such as Maureen and Chris Pianca and Simon White, a regular in the Johnny Haynes Lounge. Also there was Michael Hoodless, one of the major sponsors in George Cohen's lounge, an

enormously generous man with a great love of life and Fulham in particular. After dinner, I was asked to address a few words to the room. "It's not that many years ago," I said, "that this club was on its knees. Seats were missing in the Riverside Stand, weeds were growing on the terraces, the average gate was 4,000.

"Tomorrow we are in a European final. We have the best manager in the Premier League and the best chairman in the Premier League. We are here on the eve of Fulham's greatest ever day. Here's to tomorrow – and victory." I think everybody in the room believed we would win. We'd come through so much, the team had grown so much in confidence that the cup really did seem to have our name on it. I reported to the stadium early the following morning where my opposite number from Atletico Madrid and I were given our scripts telling us what we had to say and do during the day. Part of the plan was that thirty minutes before kick-off we would be hoisted on cranes above the goals and in front of our respective fans. From there we would warm up the supporters, each club would play a rousing song with a special meaning to its fans, and then we would read out the team line-ups, finishing with the name of the manager. Then, with ten minutes or so to kick-off, the cranes would be lowered and we would take our seats in a media area in the stand behind the dugouts. We rehearsed everything without the cranes which were not available until later.

During the lunch break I did a phone interview with Talk Sport radio, then popped over to the Channel 5 van where Colin Murray and the production team were putting together the evening's show, including my rousing poem. As the day wore on, it became clear that the weather was going to be pretty grim for May – cold and raining. Not so good on a cherry-picker, I can tell you. As it rose two tiers up in front of the stand housing our supporters, I was quickly reminded of my fear of heights. There were three of us up there. Apart from myself, there were two Germans – the crane operator and a TV cameraman who was panning between me and the crowd. There wasn't a great deal of room and one end of the crane was completely open. It went through my mind that if the cameraman whacked me by accident with the camera, I could go flying straight through the gaping hole. It would certainly be a sensational exit, or final bow, but one I wasn't ready for quite yet.

The Spanish were the first to go. As I looked at the huge screen above me, I could see what looked like a fiesta, a splash of red and white at their end of the ground as they waved their scarves in response to the voice of their announcer. Then came a rousing Eurovision-type song which they all sang along to. And then the reading of their team and a huge cheer for each of their heroes.

While all this was going on and bearing in mind my hatred of heights, I told the cameraman to inform the crane operator, who spoke no English, that the moment I announced the last name, that of the manager Roy Hodgson, he should lower the crane to the ground.

Now it was Fulham's turn. Smiling broadly, and covering the fact that I was quaking inside, I started my warm-up. The Fulham crowd in front of me sounded much louder than Atletico's, but then I was much nearer to them so I may have been mistaken. They certainly made a lot of noise. As I looked at all those faces, it struck me that we'd all come on this long journey together. This club with its quaint ground was no longer a supporting act in London football. On this night we were carrying the flag for English football. Millions of people back home, no matter which club they supported, were hoping that Fulham would win in Europe.

I rattled off the names, every one followed by a huge roar: "Number 1 – Mark Schwarzer; 2 – Chris Baird; 18 – Aaron Hughes; 5 – Brede Hangeland; 3 – Paul Konchesky; 16 – Damien Duff; 20 – Dickson Etuhu; 13 – the captain, Danny Murphy; 29 – Simon Davies; 11 – Zoltan Gera; and 25 – Bobby Zamora.

Dan Shrimpton eagerly awaits the arrival of the players while I warm up the crowd from atop the cherry-picker.

And the subs: number 19 – Pascal Zuberbühler; 4 – John Pantsil; 17 – Björn Helge Riise; 23 – Clint Dempsey; 27 – Jonathan Greening; 34 – Kagisho Digacoi; and 10 – Eric Nevland. And the Fulham manager is Roy Hodgson."

"Right," I said to the cameraman. "Let's go down." He nodded to the operator who pressed a huge button and the cage shook. For the first time I looked down and we didn't appear to be moving. A heated conversation ensued between the two Germans, of which I understood not a word. The operator pressed the button again, the cage shook even more but lowered not an inch. I glanced behind me to the other end of the ground to see the Atletico crane and its occupants back on terra firma and its announcer, a man probably not the slightest fazed by heights, heading back to the stand. By now Fulham supporters in front of me, previously so animated and friendly, were rightly getting annoyed as we were blocking their view of the opening ceremony which was under way. "Oy, David," some of them shouted. "Go forth and multiply." Or words to that effect. Suddenly, I was feeling as welcome as a bacon sandwich at a bar mitzvah.

Simon Davies (top left in this television picture) scores our thrilling equalising goal with a superb volley.

All sorts of things were going through my mind at this point. Obviously, the crane had stuck and if it remained there some of our supporters behind the goal were not going to be seeing much of the match. If I was going to get off, the only way I could think of was by rope ladder and, since my legs had already turned to jelly, that could have been pretty difficult. After what seemed like an eternity, but was probably about five minutes, the crane started slowly lowering towards the turf, operated, it turns out, by someone on the ground. I walked round the touchline in front of our supporters wearing the falsest false smile I've ever had in my life.

And so to the match. For the first half-hour Atletico Madrid looked much the better side and on 32 minutes Diego Forlan, their best player, scored their first goal. Five minutes later we were back in it when Simon Davies half volleyed Zoltan Gera's cross into the back of the net in front of the Madrid supporters. As the rain came down and the match went into extra time we started to believe that Fulham, having come this far and soaked up so much pressure, might still do it. My own feeling was that if it went to penalties, Fulham would win. But with just four minutes to go, Forlan struck again. Several Fulham players were lying on the ground. So many times on the way to Hamburg they had come back after being behind. This time they knew it was too late.

I headed back to the coach that would take us back to the hotel. I was the first on there and when I took a call on the mobile from Tony Livesey on BBC Radio Five Live, I couldn't hide the awful flat feeling you get after a disappointment like that. There was a very muted atmosphere among the players on the plane back to Gatwick the following day. It was like the '75 cup final all over again. We'd been brilliant all the way but just couldn't make it on the big day. But then we remembered. This is Fulham, a club that wouldn't exist were it not for the efforts of those people behind Fulham 2000 and the generosity of Mohamed Al Fayed. We'd just been in a European final and next season would be our tenth in the Premier League, our longest ever run in the top division in England.

Come on, you Whites!

Chapter 28

Voice of Anfield

In April 2010, a letter arrived at Craven Cottage addressed to me by George Sephton, who for forty years – yes, forty years! – has been the 'Voice of Anfield'. "Had I seen the Liverpool v Fulham programme for the match on April 10?" Actually, I hadn't and no-one had told me about it. Luckily, he enclosed a copy and in it was an article that was enormously flattering both to him and me but also said a lot about the esteem in which Fulham is held by even the biggest clubs. Under the heading 'Proudly announcing the two Greatest Matchday Voices', Chris McLoughlin, after some scathing remarks about some other clubs and how not to do it, came to the conclusion that "when it comes to the crème-de-la-crème of PA announcers, we've got one of the runners in a two-horse race. In the red corner is George Sephton, the Voice of Anfield since 1972, and in the white corner is Fulham's Diddy David Hamilton, the voice of Craven Cottage since 1996."

George was thrilled, and so was I to be placed on a par with a man who'd been doing the job at a top club for so long. In the article this is what Chris McLoughlin said about Fulham: "The cost of a ticket apart, I love going to Fulham. It's the best ground in London, a proper ground that oozes history and tradition in every corner, not just the Cottage itself." There – that's what someone thinks of us at one of the top clubs. He went on to say, "Fulham is a family club and when Diddy David speaks over the microphone it's like he's addressing 20,000 people he knows rather than a faceless crowd in a soulless bowl who can't hear him speak over the crunching of lobster and the popping of corks."

It was nice of Chris to compliment us in this way but I'm sure George would agree that the nub of what we do is saying the right thing at the right time. It isn't anything you can write on a script and it's very easy to say the wrong thing at the wrong time, like the announcer at a Welsh club who said of an opposing player, "Coming on now is number 10, Junior Bent, and he probably is." Or the mike man at a major London club who said to the players of a lower league club in a cup game, "Enjoy your big day out. Next week you'll be playing

THE ANNIE ROAD CORNER

The thing about **US** and **THEM** is...

Proudly announcing the two greatest matchday voices

Fulham's 'Diddy' David and our own George Sephton help set the right tone

The Twe12th Man

DEPENDING on what you read, it was either legendary Brazilian midfielder Didi or raconteur extraordinaire Stuart Hall who first described football as "the beautiful game."

Watching Brazil play it can be a [...] and so too can [...] escribe it, because [...] bout wha[...]

music is played, and what is said over the PA System, before a match has even kicked off.

Take Middlesbrough, for instance, where it seems the only uplifting moment the locals enjoy amidst plooms of grey smoke is the ritualistic clapping along to that annoying 'der der der der,' [...] team run out to.

Above: Boro fans love to cheer their team out to a rather annoying ditty

George and me, as we appeared in the Liverpool programme.

in front of three thousand again." A big club being patronising to a small one. Not on, in my book.

Since George Sephton first contacted me, we've been in regular touch and I had hoped we might meet up at the Europa League final in Hamburg. Sadly, Liverpool didn't quite make it, beaten in the semi-final by Atletico Madrid, just one game away from an all-England final. Shame, because George could have been on that other cherry-picker! One of these days I'm hoping he might come down to Craven Cottage, or perhaps I'll go up to Anfield. Naturally, we have compared notes and one difference we've spotted is that he still plays the music on match days and I don't. Oh yes, and that song. When Gerry and the Pacemakers recorded *You'll Never Walk Alone,* what a gift they gave to Liverpool Football Club! The nearest we ever had to our own song was *Viva El Fulham* in 1975 and that sounds a bit dated now. But still every time I hear *You'll Never Walk Alone* it brings out the goose bumps. A real football anthem, and worth three points to the team.

Writing of Liverpool brings me to Roy Hodgson who, following our great run in Europe, couldn't resist the temptation to go there, the chance to manage what has always been regarded as one of our major clubs. As with Kevin Keegan before him, leaving Fulham turned out not to be a good move. The thing was that Roy was so right for Fulham and Fulham was so right for him. What works at one club doesn't necessarily work at another. In Roy's place came Mark Hughes. I met him briefly at Mohamed Al Fayed's leaving party at Harrods shortly after he joined the club. He seemed very friendly and in his one season at the club he took Fulham to 8th in the Premier League, their second best finish. When he departed with his coaching team whom I nicknamed 'The Tafia' (Welsh mafia) it came as a shock to everybody, and an even bigger shock was that he didn't have another job to go to, but it left the club with the opportunity to appoint Martin Jol, the man they wanted in the first place. He would be the man to lead Fulham into their eleventh Premier League season and, thanks to the Fair Play League, another crack at Europe.

George Sephton will be pleased to know that grand-daughter Allie has announced that she's a Liverpool fan! Hopefully, it's just a phase.

Dreena, me and Max, the football fan.

Chapter 29

It's Me or the Dog

In 2004 my dog, Max, was featured on the TV programme *It's Me Or The Dog*. Max is a Gordon setter, which is a rare breed. Gordon setters are usually black and tan, but Max is liver and tan which makes him even rarer. He isn't a bad dog. In fact, he's good natured and particularly tolerant with children who might want to pull his ears or his tail. But he is eccentric. Part of his eccentricity may stem from the fact that prior to joining the Hamilton household he was a regimental mascot in Scotland. During his time with the Army he was run over by a lorry and finished up in the vet's hospital with two broken legs and who knows what other injuries. All of this has left him somewhat loopy. When his regiment was posted abroad, he returned to the breeder who persuaded us that we would provide the right kind of household for a dog who was barking in more ways than one.

As we swiftly discovered, Max is heavily into mirrors. (I know, it runs in the family.) After his appearance on television, Channel 4 were swamped with enquiries from people asking how they could get a liver and tan Gordon setter, which rather defeated the object of the programme.

Naturally, I watch a lot of football on TV, often with Max sitting at my feet. One day, and I promise you this is true, he stood up, looked at the screen and started following the progress of the ball. He was slightly confused when there was a cut-away shot of a player and the ball disappeared, but when it went past the post he shot round to the back of the television set to see where it had gone to.

One day my wife came into the room, caught Max watching the game and said to me, "Trust you to have a dog who likes football."

"Knowing my luck," I said, "he's probably a bloody Chelsea supporter."

From the picture album

Pre-match banter with the chairman.

From the picture album

On the town with Gloria Hunniford and Victor Spinetti.

Sir Roger Moore visits my radio studio – 007 and 006½.

Chapter 30

When Piers Came to Fulham

Hugh Grant and I were among those who appeared in a video tribute to Mohamed Al Fayed which was played at the chairman's leaving party at Harrods. On it Hugh thanked the chairman for allowing him to share his blanket on cold days at Craven Cottage. I offered my thanks to Mohamed for all his helpful suggestions of what I might like to do with my microphone during our pre-match chats.

Since he is a showman himself, the chairman obviously enjoys the company of show business folk. His friendship with Piers Morgan goes back to the days when Piers was the editor of the *Daily Mirror*. Though Piers is an Arsenal fan, he does enjoy his visits to Craven Cottage and his repartee with our leader. On one such occasion, the chairman introduced me to Piers on the touchline. "Do you know David Hamilton?" he asked.

"Indeed I do," said Piers. "We've played tennis together." Very kindly he didn't mention the score.

Piers was not as modest when filming a TV show with Cliff

Hugh Grant is excited to meet the world-famous Les Strong on the Fulham pitch.

Richard at Cliff's luxurious home in Barbados. As they headed to Cliff's tennis court, Piers told him, "I've only played against two celebrities before – Chris Evans and Diddy David Hamilton – and I thrashed them both."

In my case, I have to admit he was right. So what was the score? He beat me 6–2, 6–1 and, to be honest, by the second set I was lucky to get 1. A couple of days later pictures appeared in his newspaper column of Piers looking triumphant and me looking knackered. It was only some time afterwards that I discovered Piers was a county champion. He kept that pretty quiet. As anyone who's come up against him would know, he's a very competitive man, but he really should change his football club.

Tennis ace Piers Morgan.

Chapter 31

Gentleman George

The George Cohen Lounge on the ground floor of the Riverside Stand is decorated with photographs from his illustrious career. There's the famous one of Sir Alf Ramsey refusing to allow George to swap shirts with an Argentinian player after the England manager had called them 'animals'. There's one of George being tackled by George Best (yes, I did get that the right

Gentleman George and I in front of a famous photograph – one of the many that adorn the George Cohen Lounge. In the picture Alf Ramsey refuses to let George swap shirts after the match against Argentina. Sir Alf was disgusted by their tactics.

way round) and another of George walking out proudly behind Bobby Moore before the '66 World Cup final.

On match days the lounge has an atmosphere of bonhomie created by genial George and his lovely wife, Daphne. Where George goes, Daphne goes – as solid a marriage as you will ever see. Our Q and A sessions after the game have been pure joy. I've learned so much about the game by listening to a man who's played it at the highest level. George is also a very honest character, and when the team have been doing badly and he's reluctant to criticise the club who are paying his wages, he becomes George the diplomat, while not compromising his credibility, a difficult juggling act. When they're doing well, no-one is more pleased.

For our post-match chat we've often been joined by celebrity supporters from visiting teams as well as George's former colleagues and DJ and pop group friends of mine. If John Motson is commentating, he often drops in for a brandy after the game. They all love to chat to George and he's always pleased to see them. Something that's almost unique about those sessions is that there's never any bad language, and that's the way George likes it. We might have the odd risqué joke, but the only time I heard the f-word was when David Speedie was a guest and peppered the afternoon with it. I don't think he's been back.

Ask George who was the best winger he ever played against and he'll say Cliff Jones, the Welsh international who played for Spurs. "You couldn't mark him out of the game," George told me. "Whatever you did, he would counter it. He was brave, very fast with the ball, two-footed and lethal at the far post with headers." Cliff finished his career playing alongside George at Fulham. Sadly, by then his best days were over, but the two of them remain great friends. "Whenever I see him," said George, "he gives me a big hug and says, 'That's the closest you ever got to me.' "

Despite his genial personality, George was a tough, strong player and it was that physical strength that helped him win his long battle against cancer after he finished playing. But he's never lost his sense of humour, as regulars to his lounge like Michael Hoodless and Bob Howes will attest, and it's often quite self-deprecating. He once told me about a journey he had on the London Underground. George was strap-hanging, and sitting in front of him was an attractive young woman. As she stood up and came towards him, George's hand headed towards his breast pocket, preparing to attend to the usual autograph request. At which point the lady said, "Would you like my seat?" To a former professional sportsman, this must have come as quite a shock, but George saw the funny side of it.

After one match we were in the lounge having our photos taken with some sponsors who'd travelled up from the south coast for the game. Standing

An artist's impression of our double act.

between us was a young woman who'd had a fair amount to drink and was, shall we say, in a fairly jolly mood. Suddenly, I was aware of her hand massaging my bottom. I glanced across at George who had an enormous smile on his face. "Is the same thing happening to you that's happening to me?" I asked him. George nodded and carried on smiling for the camera. Afterwards we laughed at the fact that even at our 'veteran' stage someone still gets some enjoyment out of feeling our bums.

Visitors to George's lounge can always be assured of hearing his recollections of 1966 and his stories of Nobby Stiles and Jack and Bobby Charlton. Most of all they enjoy his convivial company over lunch where he really is 'the host with the most'. Gentleman George is a true legend and surely it can only be a matter of time before Daphne becomes Lady Cohen.

From the picture album

On *The One Show* with fellow DJs
Tony Blackburn, Trevor Nelson, Mike
Read and David Jensen.

*Let's Dance for Sport Relief, 2012. Tony Blackburn
and I trip the (not so) light fantastic. Rehearsals at
Elstree started well when Ali, the choreographer,
greeted me with the words: "My father-in-law John
Lewis is a pal of yours. He's a Fulham supporter!"*

*Peter Foot, chairman of the Campaign For
Courtesy, presents a certificate acknowledging
the exemplary behaviour of Fulham fans to
David Lloyd, editor of TOOFIF, DH, Les Strong,
Matthew Lloyd and Martin Plumb.*

From the picture album

On ITV's Loose Women in February 2012, Janet Street-Porter tells me she's a lifelong Fulham fan. I offer to put her on the pitch at half-time. "What, like a mascot?" she asks, so I offer to introduce her to Billy the Badger.

Introducing the great Johnny Haynes to the Fulham crowd in April 2002. What a privilege!

From the scrapbook

Fulham fans boost funds

FULHAM 2000 has exceeded a £200,000 target set for the start of the season after fans' huge response since the fundraising campaign's launch in March.

The campaign, hoped to raise £1 million to keep Fulham FC at Craven Cottage before a 1996 deadline set by landlords The Royal Bank of Scotland, has received £210,000 from supporters.

The news follows newspaper reports claiming Chelsea's Pitch Owners Scheme ran at an operating loss in its first year despite raising almost £300,000 from selling shares.

Chelsea have blamed the £79,000 cost of setting up the Chelsea Pitch Owners company for the operating balance.

Fulham 2000 Chairman Melvin Tenner now believes a £500,000 target for the start of the 1995-6 season is realistic.

He said: "We hope to double our money in a year's time. We are going outside the club for the first time to launch a wider campaign."

Fulham 2000 chairman Melvin Tenner, David Hamilton and Fulham chairman Jimmy Hill at the fundraising campaign launch

Fulham Chronicle

Fulham and Hammersmith Chronicle

How the Fulham crowd booed their team off at the interval. Jol tore into his players at the break and sent them out early. 'I told them to be more direct,' he said with a scowl.

But few neutrals would have done anything but scoff at David Hamilton, the former Radio One DJ who now does the stadium announcing by the Thames, when he said: 'Well, the boys are out early, they really mean business, so let's get behind them.'

It almost sounded pitiful ... but perhaps he knew something the rest of us did not. Twenty three minutes later Fulham had scored four and the game was over

Mail On Sunday

Sao Paulo to the Cottage – for £700

YOUR favourite local paper raised nearly £1,000 for charity at a sportsman's dinner held by Fulham FC.

The event at a Heathrow hotel was staged to celebrate the Whites' 100th anniversary as a professional club.

Among the guests were Fulham manager Kevin Keegan, World Cup winner George Cohen, Fulham legend Gordon 'Ivor' Davies, and Bobby Moore's widow Suzanne.

All the diners were presented with a complimentary copy of *Fulham Chronicled*, this paper's special 16-page supplement produced to mark the club's birthday.

Around 150 revellers were entertained by after-dinner speaker, former Liverpool star and television presenter Ian St John.

Fulham's match day MC David Hamilton was the auctioneer at a sale of football memorabilia.

Among the items on sale were two letters congratulating the club on its birthday from Tony Blair and footballing legend Pelé.

Both were received by this paper for *Fulham Chronicled* and we donated them for the auction which was raising cash for the Bobby Moore Fund for Imperial Cnacer Research.

The Prime Minister's signature fetched £275, but Pelé raised a fantastic £700 – the highest bid of the night.

Fulham manager Kevin Keegan and David Hamilton enjoy their copy of our special supplement *Fulham Chronicled*

Pic: JAMES ELLIS

Fulham find themselves in panto season

LYRIC Theatre pantomime dame Sarah the cook was the half-time entertainment in front of 25,000 football fans at Craven Cottage on Sunday.

Fulham FC fans needed some cheering up during the interval of their Premier League clash with moneybags Manchester City, as they were losing 3-0.

So Sarah, embarking on a series of public appearances to plug the theatre's Christmas panto Dick Whittington and his Cat, took to the pitch with club announcer David Hamilton and mascot Billy the Badger.

The show at the theatre, in Lyric Square, begins tomorrow (Saturday) with residents of the borough or people who work in Hammersmith and Fulham able to bag free tickets. All you have to do claim four tickets is provide proof of your address or employment to the ticket office before 7pm on Saturday.

The panto runs until January 8. Tickets cost between £10 and £25. Call 08712 211 722 or visit www.lyric.co.uk.

■ WINNING RECIPE: Sarah the cook, David Hamilton and Billy the badger   Contributed

Fulham Gazette

Chapter 32

Half-time

Three times my home has been featured on *Through The Keyhole* – my house in Barnes twice (once for BBC, once ITV) and my present home in Sussex once. Each time there has been a Fulham clue – a ceramic of Craven Cottage, a Fulham shirt or an aerial shot of the ground. In one edition Sir David Frost picked up on the fact that on the coffee table in the sitting-room was a copy of Ken Coton's tome, *Fulham's Golden Years*. "Must be a very short book," quipped Eamonn Holmes.

Eamonn is one of many celebrities who've been on the Craven Cottage pitch to do the half-time draw of what for many years was the highly popular Fulham Flutter. Often it was made by glamorous ladies like Linda Lusardi, Scorpio (from the TV series *Gladiators)*, Michelle Collins and, early in her career, an up-and-coming model and actress called Jordan.

DJ Mike Read caused quite a stir when he did the draw. As he walked on to the pitch, he said to me, "While I'm on here, I'd love to kick a ball."

"Stay around," I said. "You may get a chance later."

The next item was a competition between Fulham and Portsmouth supporters, three from each side kicking from their end of the ground to see who could get the ball nearest to a mat in the centre circle. The prize for the winner was a home cinema.

The first contestant was a woman from Portsmouth who took her kick from near the goalpost. As the ball headed towards the half-way line, Mike suddenly left my side, ran across the pitch and booted it into touch. The Portsmouth crowd, never the quietest at away grounds, were yelling abuse at him and a steward dragged him away. (Mike later claimed he couldn't hear what I was saying and didn't realise a competition was taking place.) Fortunately, each contestant was given a second attempt at it, and with her second shot the woman from Portsmouth got nearest to the target and won the home cinema. It was the only time I was glad to see a half-time contest won by an away fan. Afterwards I pulled Mike's leg, saying that he had been banned from appearing on the pitch again. I think he half believed me.

Holding a Fulham umbrella, Michael Jackson greets a stunned Craven Cottage crowd in April 1999. Fulham chairman Mohamed Al Fayed gets ready to swirl his scarf in celebration.

Before the arrival of Mohamed Al Fayed, the half-time guests were stars rather than superstars, which is perhaps why the crowd were caught out when Fulham's most famous guest came visiting on April 10, 1999. Shortly before he

arrived, I'd been tipped off: "Michael Jackson is here. Get ready to introduce him to the crowd." Suddenly he appeared, holding a black and white umbrella over his head even though it was a hot, sunny day.

"Ladies and gentlemen," I said. "Please welcome the one, the only Michael Jackson." He walked around the touchline to what I can only describe as polite applause. I reckon people thought it was a gag, that he was a lookalike. Then, as he came round to the Stevenage Road Stand, the penny dropped. As people realised it

Tony Macedo

Roger Brown – a colossus in both defence and attack.

Jimmy Hill

was the real Michael Jackson, the applause turned into an ovation.

When Tony Curtis arrived a few months later, the crowd didn't make the same mistake. This time they reacted immediately, and Curtis responded by leaping up several rows into the Hammersmith End Stand.

Over the years we've had all kinds of half-time entertainment: singers, dancers, ball jugglers. What goes down best is when Fulham legends appear, particularly if the crowd haven't seen them for a while. Goalkeeper Ian Black came back at the age of 82, still looking fit and sprightly. His successor, Tony Macedo, who played nearly 400 times for the club, returned to the Cottage in 2011 for the first time in 43 years and came out on to the pitch to a standing ovation. It was a moving occasion for Tony who was almost in tears.

Another man who came out with tears in his eyes was Jimmy Hill, who had given so much to the club both as player and manager and who loves Craven Cottage more than even he could describe. His enormous contribution to Fulham should never be forgotten.

Tosh Chamberlain is always welcome with his cheeky, bubbly personality. Terry Angus went down a storm as did Rufus Brevett, Simon Morgan, Jimmy Conway, over from the States, who came on the pitch with his brother John who played alongside him at Fulham, and Roger Brown, who came to visit not long before he died far too young in 2011.

I have to admit it makes my life easier if the team are winning, or at least drawing, at the interval, though the crowd have been incredibly good natured when things haven't been going so well in the first half. It was tough on the pantomime dame from the Lyric Theatre, Hammersmith, who was due on at half-time when we were being severely drubbed by Manchester City. I resisted the temptation to say, "It's panto time," knowing that instead of a "Oh, no it isn't!" I might have got an "Oh, yes it is!"

Quite often I've been asked to read out marriage proposals. Since the answer is usually "Yes", you can be pretty sure the crowd will burst into their song: "You don't know what you're doing."

THE ANNOUNCER

The job: Fulham's matchday announcer
Name: David Hamilton **Age:** 73

How did a Radio One icon end up at Craven Cottage?

I first went to Fulham at the age of nine because my mother lived in a flat just by Putney Bridge station. In the '70s I was a director there for a few years under Ernie Clay, who nearly ran the club into the ground. I asked to see the books one day but he refused so I resigned; I was working for the BBC at the time and didn't want any bad publicity. Then 16 years ago I was asked to become the man on the mic when the guy who did the half-time announcements left.

You've been a good luck charm too...

I suppose you could say that, yes. It was Christmas 1996 when I started the job, and at the end of the season we were promoted under Micky Adams. The following season, Mohamed al Fayed took over. I started doing all the pre-match work before I began hosting one of the lounges with George Cohen. When Mohamed al Fayed arrived he said he wanted to get the club to the Premier League in five seasons – and we did it in four.

It has been some rise – what has been the highlight?

There are so many, but the Europa League nights under Roy Hodgson [right], when we reached the final, were amazing.

Were you at that 2010 final?

I certainly was. Myself and my counterpart from Atletico Madrid were flown out to Hamburg to entertain fans before the game. They put us up on cherry-pickers but mine got stuck. I'm not very good with heights and there I was, 15 minutes before a European final, stuck several tiers up in the air. I was supposed to be warming up the crowd but it was freezing up there! I ended up getting to where I was due to be five minutes before kick-off.

Talk us through your matchday...

If it's a 3pm kick-off I'll get to the press office at 1.30pm and someone will give me a script with all the announcements and everything they want me to talk about that afternoon. I'll get over to the fourth official's dugout, test the mic and start going through my notes. I start talking 40 minutes before kick-off, then I'll sign off before the start of the game by saying, "Ladies and gentlemen... it's showtime."

Any announcements you particularly enjoy?

It has to be the marriage proposals. I'll pop the question, then get feedback on whether the woman in question says yes or no. If it's a 'yes' the whole of Craven Cottage starts singing spontaneously, "You don't know what you're doing!"

> "It was 15 minutes before the Europa League final, and I was stuck on a cherry-picker"

Four Four Two magazine, January 2012.

From the picture album

Introducing the chairman at the unveiling of
the Maestro's statue. There were gasps from
the crowd when they saw how lifelike it was.

From the scrapbook

FULHAM FLUTTER

We are still looking for the supporter who has **ticket number 1100** from Tuesday nights Flutter. If you have this ticket, **you have until 5pm today to claim the £300 from Mark Rouse.**

FULHAM LOTTERIES

5 lucky people have now won £1,500

Don't forget to get involved before Les Strong draws today's lucky number

David Hamilton tastes the winnings before handing it over to our latest Flutter winner

≫ fulham folk

a behind-the-scenes glimpse at the people that make your club tick. this week, matchday mc, david hamilton…

So David, how did you first come to work for the Club?

Well it all happened 13 years ago, when I was asked if I could do the half-time entertainment having spent many years in the showbiz environment. I did that for a few months, then at the end of the season the Club's announcer left so I started to do that as well. I also became a days, his stints on Top of the Pops and his Thames Television link-man role plus, of

The Sunderland game was your 300th match as the Club's matchday MC, how did that feel, especially having celebrated the landmark on such a momentous day?

It was quite a day. To be honest it was obviously Johnny Haynes' day – and rightly so, but it was a great occasion all round. Before the game I compered the unveiling of the statue, which I have to describe your 13 ?

Apart from battling with relegation of late - which has been bad for the old ticker - it's been absolutely fantastic. I really have loved every minute of it. I'm right down on the touchline, so I feel every tackle and hear every shout. I can't help but feel part of what's going on. I really do have the best seat in the house!

Having worked in both television and radio, you've always enjoyed a career in the spotlight, but how do you deal with walking out in front of 20,000+ fans, something that would daunt most of us?

saturday november 15th
ulham v tottenham hotspur   69

Fratton Park are a joy to watch.

I was also delighted to hear the distinctive tones of our own David Hamilton 'topping

course, his time with the inimitable Ken Dodd that led to his nickname of "Diddy". I trust Diddy has no plans to invite "Doddy" along to the Cottage as a half-time guest – if he got hold of the mike we'd never get the second half under way!

I sincerely hope that our winning run in those last few games of last season will serve as something of a springboard for our 2008-09 campaign. And that Diddy David Hamilton's professional tones will continue to add some polish to the Craven Cottage matchday entertainment.

'Jimmy Dunne's shorts'

The Ed replies: As the pic on Page 5 shows, I bumped into David Hamilton during the close season at a function. W told me (no sources, ab not the done Les Strong!) his 300th ma

Taking the pitch! David Hamilton is flanked by FFC legends Tosh Chamberlain (left) and Ian Black.
Pic: Keith Crosswell (Encore magazine)

FRIENDS OF FULHAM

David Hamilton

DIDDY DAVES DISCO

RIVERSIDE SUITE
SATURDAY, 25th OCTOBER
7.30 —— 12.00

together with "C.G.R. ROADSHOW"

Friends of Fulham £1.00 (Inc. VAT)
Non-Members £1.25 (Inc. VAT)

Last year's disco with David Hamilton was a sell out and we turned people away at the door on the evening. Make sure you do not miss out this year by applying now by post (please enclose S.A.E.). There will be no admission on the door on the evening and, regrettably, no admission for under-18's.

TWO FULLY-STOCKED BARS ★ GIANT RAFFLE ★ REFRESHMENTS AVAILABLE

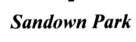

David Hamilton
at
Variety Club Day
-
Sandown Park
-
Saturday
20th August 2005

Chapter 33

Full Time

The Fulham Football Club of today is very different from the one I knew as a boy. The players no longer train at Craven Cottage – the running track around the pitch is long gone – and you're not likely to catch them strolling through Bishops Park or in the local pub at lunchtime. The chairman isn't a comedian, players won't stay as long at the club and won't have testimonials any more, and more of them will come from foreign countries. Supporters have become more partisan. Few now go to Fulham one week and Chelsea the next, but those in the game who seek to make it more tribal should be wary lest it comes back and bites them on the bum. Season after season Fulham top the league of the best behaved supporters in the Premier League, a record we can feel justly proud of.

The game itself has changed greatly since my schooldays. Then teams lined up with five forwards – outside right, inside right, centre forward, inside left and outside left – three half-backs and two full-backs. Incredible to think that instead of 4–4–2, the formation was 2–3–5. More women go to football now and more of them work at football clubs. In Ernie Clay's days women were not allowed in the boardroom, and wives, girlfriends and daughters had tea in a different room. My daughter often served it for them. Instead of Honor Blackman and Harry Fowler (who died in January 2012, aged 85), the celebrities you may see in the stand will be Hugh Grant and Keith and Lily Allen. Hugh, incidentally, was there long before the glory years and once sponsored the kit of the goalkeeper 'Big' Jim Stannard.

Many familiar faces, both on and off the pitch, have gone far too young. Fulham's favourite son, Johnny Haynes, died after a car crash in Edinburgh on his 71st birthday in October 2005. An unassuming and modest man, he was always a welcome visitor to the Cottage though his visits were far too rare since he chose to live a long way away, first in South Africa and then in Edinburgh. The Maestro lives on with his statue in Stevenage Road, surely one of the finest

Opposite: an Alan Williams montage of pictures he took at a Variety Club of Great Britain race meeting at Sandown Park. (See next page about Alan.)

Jimmy Hill and club secretary Graham Hortop welcome Fulham supporter Honor Blackman and her husband Maurice Kaufman to the Cottage.

statues of a footballer anywhere, sculpted by Douglas Jennings. I was proud to MC the unveiling ceremony by Mohamed Al Fayed in October 2008.

In recent times that one minute's silence has come round too often. Bedford Jezzard in 2005, just five months before Johnny Haynes, George Best a month after Johnny in November 2005, Jim Langley in December 2007, Arthur Stevens also in 2007.

In May 2010, we lost Alan Williams, the man who had been such a driving force behind Fulham 2000. One of the last of a breed of old-fashioned bank managers, Alan was also an outstanding photographer and months after he died, his wife Beryl ensured the publication of his book *Flash Bang Wallop*, an incredible collection of pictures by the self-styled 'Photographer to the Stars'. Some of his photos are also included in this book. Alan's funeral service was conducted by the Fulham FC chaplain, the Reverend Gary Piper, and George Cohen and I were among those who paid our tributes.

Also, literally, from the old school was Peter Thomson, the headmaster of the Harrodian School and a Fulham fanatic who died in May 2011. An estimated 1,500 people attended a thanksgiving service for him at St. Paul's Church, Hammersmith. Peter was not a typical football supporter, but he was a typical Fulham supporter. The club were lucky to have him because he wrote a wonderful series of books, Following The Fulham, published by Ashwater Press.

At a reception following the service I bumped into the attractive actress Sharon Duce, once one of Fulham's celebrity supporters along with her husband, Dominic Guard. She told me that she stopped coming to Fulham after Micky Adams was dispensed with but instead had remained friendly with Micky and had followed him to various clubs around the country. I admired her loyalty but felt that having been there through the tough years, she had denied herself the successful ones. Two different ways of looking at things, I suppose.

There are many good people the club is lucky to have. Dennis Turner, the club's historian, writer of so many fine books about Fulham – and a brilliant after dinner speaker – is now rightly a member of the board, as are Michael Cole, whom I worked with at Anglia Television, and Mark Collins, very much a link between old Fulham and new. Ken Coton, Fulham's photographer over five decades, has the most incredible archive of pictures, many of which have appeared in Fulham books published by his company, Ashwater Press, frequently with words by another Fulham devotee, Martin Plumb. Gary Piper is a familiar figure known to all the players at the training ground and on hand should any of them need his counsel, and is also to be found in charge of the ball boys on match day, a constant presence at the club for more years than he cares to remember – as much a part of the furniture as Ray Lewington, who has been at Fulham for over 30 years as player, player-manager, manager, assistant manager and coach. He told me he's done everything, including making the tea.

Sandra Coles has run the ticket office with a smile for nigh on 40 years, and then there's Gentleman Jim McGullian, commentator at the Cottage and away from home, whose return journeys must have been long after watching a team that in the last few years haven't been the best of travellers. Add to the list matchday photographer Baz Seal, Alan Blackmore, who looks after the mascots (thanks for all the laughs, guys, on the touchline), and those unsung heroes, the paramedics. All these people, I've discovered, don't just work for Fulham, they love the club and wouldn't want to be doing the job anywhere else. It's not just a job, more a way of life. Wherever I go, I bump into Fulham supporters. It's like one big family that stretches all over the world. I can be in a bar somewhere and someone will come over and talk about Fulham.

Among the supporters, I've got to know people like Barbara Davidson who's followed the club for over 75 years and in recent times has been involved in fundraising for the Community Sports Trust. All the Fulham players came to her 21st birthday in 1950, and Les Strong, George Cohen, Mark Collins and I were among those at her 80th birthday party in 2009 when the chairman gave her a diamond-encrusted cashmere shawl. A true lifetime fan.

The man whose family has been around the longest must be David Shrimpton. His grandfather Henry captained Fulham and claimed to be the first man to kick a ball at Craven Cottage, back in 1896. Three of his brothers

Barbara Davidson, lifetime Fulham fan, and brilliant reader of the game.

played for Fulham. David himself became a director in 1991 and, along with Bill Muddyman, was one of the people responsible for bringing Mohamed Al Fayed to the club.

My own family are ardent Fulham supporters. My son, David junior, has a season ticket in the Riverside Stand. (David is a writer on the *Daily Express* so the by-line David Pilditch appears under headlines as it did all those years ago in *Soccer Star*.) My daughter Jane and granddaughter Allie get to games as often as they can, as do my stepson Simon and his son Sam. Sam did a Fulham junior training course at Motspur Park and is turning into a decent player. My stepdaughter Charlotte booked her daughter Issy into the Fulham FC summer camp at

Rosemary and David Shrimpton get their hands on silverware – the Division Two championship trophy in May 1999.

Jane, my daughter, served the tea in the directors' room and learned a new vocabulary from George Best's wife, Angie. David, my son, is a journalist on the Daily Express. Born in Manchester, he shed a few tears when Man U were beaten by Arsenal in the cup final. He's cried more since I persuaded him to change his allegiance to Fulham.

Hurlingham Park, which she thoroughly enjoyed. When Issy comes to visit she enjoys a kick-about with Sam's sister Ciara and my other stepdaughter Angela's children Lily, Beau and Rafe. That's another generation of Fulham fans in the making. Among Angie and Craig's best friends are Jonathan Greening and his wife Anna.

Fulham have gold dust in the legends who host the lounges on match days. As well as George Cohen, whom I work with, there's Alan Mullery in the Chairman's Lounge. A Fulham and England captain no less and nowadays a pundit on Sky, Alan has definite and forthright views on the game and is a witty and clever raconteur. Les Strong is another funny man and his double act with Tony Gale is one of the highlights of the Johnny Haynes Lounge in the Riverside Stand. Freddie Callaghan, one of the most genuine people I've ever met, holds court with a loyal bunch of followers in the Riverside Restaurant. The one legend on the other side of the ground is the ever popular Gordon Davies, Fulham's all-time top goalscorer, having beaten the previous record set by Johnny Haynes. 'Ivor' today is the host in the Maestro's Lounge.

David Lloyd, George Cohen and I try to come up with the right answers on the TV show Taking the Pitch.

I must also mention Anne Holmes and Debbie Maynard, the hostesses in George and Alan's lounges. Simply the best. And what would Fulham be without the sight of David Lloyd at his pitch in Stevenage Road, clutching copies of *There's Only One F in Fulham*, his award winning fanzine? Despite the demands of bringing up a large family, David has edited *TOOFIF* for 24 years, bringing to it a standard of journalism any newspaper would be happy to achieve, and despite the advent of internet forums where people can have their say immediately, the fanzine retains a healthy and loyal readership. Because of its reputation, David's views on Fulham are often sought by press, radio and TV.

Football today is big business. Supporters may find it hard to understand that Jimmy Bullard and Louis Saha should move on to clubs they think are bigger or who might pay them more, but it's a short life. There aren't many jobs where you are retired or finished at 35. And not many players will go on to become successful managers. Players and managers today don't have the same feelings about clubs or the same loyalty as supporters do. While they inevitably move on, we fans are here for life. Fulham till I die.

How would it have been if Mohamed Al Fayed hadn't come along? I dread to think. What a time it's been. Three promotions, our longest ever run in the

Dreena's boy Simon and his son, Sam – two more generations of Fulham fans.

top division, our highest ever league place and a European final. One day we may look back on these as Fulham's golden years. As Tommy Trinder would have said, "You lucky people!" Even Tommy would have to concede that Mohamed Al Fayed is without doubt the most successful chairman in the club's long history.

Looking at the DVD of Fulham's 2001 season, celebrating our Premiership promotion (released at Christmas 2011), I was reminded of how lethal Louis Saha, Luis Boa Morte and Barry Hayles were in front of goal and how hungry they were for the ball. In 2012 I can see the same qualities in Moussa Dembélé, Bryan Ruiz and the Russian, Pavel Pogrebnyak (now there's a challenging name to pronounce!). Plus there's the promise of Kerim Frei, the youngster who came through the academy team, coached so superbly by Kit Symonds. Waiting in the wings is another academy youngster, Marcello Trotta, who scored eight goals in eight games, including a hat trick, while out on loan at Wycombe Wanderers. The academy looks like bringing more players into the first team squad than ever before. All this bodes well for the future.

That's me with Freddie, Strongie and Mullers, three Fulham legends – but look who's got the ball!

The club that refused to die is fit and well. An announcement in 2011 of plans to increase the seating in the Riverside Stand made it clear, once and for all, that despite the uncertainty in the past, the club's future lies at Craven Cottage. As more and more clubs leave their traditional homes for bigger stadiums that totally lack any kind of character, the Cottage becomes an even more precious gem.

Quirky, unique, capricious it may be, but people love coming here. As my own final whistle draws near, I'm glad I chose it as my club all those years ago, and I'm glad to have been part of the rollercoaster journey that has brought it to where it is today.

Bob Howes, Alex Shooter and me at Fulham's Open Training Day. Craven Cottage, 2012.

My All-Time Great Fulham XI

George Cohen

Mark Schwarzer

Jimmy Langley

Alan Mullery

Brede Hangeland

Bobby Moore

Graham Leggat   Bobby Robson   Gordon Davies   Johnny Haynes   Les Barrett

SUBSTITUTES

Louis Saha   Edwin van der Sar   Chris Coleman   Tony Gale*   Les Strong**

*Fulham's greatest uncapped player.   ** To liven up the bench.

WELCOMING COTTAGE IS HOUSE OF FUN

from Chris Goreham, Eastern Daily Press, 4th April 2012

AS WITH ANY Norwich City supporter who remembers that 6–0 defeat in 2005, Craven Cottage was a place that I struggled to feel kindly about.

So it was surprising to be there on Saturday, without all that '*Survival Sunday*' nonsense, with much less sweaty palms and realise just what a quirky place it is to watch Premier League football.

The stewards were incredibly helpful on arrival. Unable to let bygones be bygones, I decided that this must be because they still felt guilty about kicking us out of the top flight in such ignominious fashion seven years ago but as I was shown to my rickety old seat those cynical feelings about all things Fulham finally started to disappear.

I had forgotten just what a great old fashioned football ground it is. In these days of all-seater enormodome style stadiums that look like they come from the same box of Meccano and have sponsors names in the title it was so refreshing to be sat in a wooden stand.

Then there was Mohamed Al Fayed's extraordinary entrance. The chairman was announced onto the pitch before the game and marched out of the tunnel to a standing ovation while he twirled his black and white scarf as if it was the chequered flag at Silverstone. The pumping soundtrack over the PA made it feel like he was stepping up to the oche in the World Darts Championship rather than taking his seat in the director's box.

The fun doesn't end there. It is terrifically surreal to have 'Diddy' David Hamilton reading out the team line-ups. The former Radio 1 DJ and *Top of the Pops* presenter is Fulham's official matchday announcer.

Even at the age of 73, his dulcet tones cut through the crackly tannoy to make the identity of today's match mascots sound almost as important as the top 10 used to be.

His broadcasting heyday may have gone but he can certainly cope with the demands of modern day Premier League football.

I wish I had been able to be as cool on Saturday when faced with what must have been English football's most complicated substitution of all time. I stumbled, stuttered and floundered while in the background 'Diddy' calmly told the crowd: "Substitution for Fulham. Coming off, number 7 Pavel Pogrebnyak and coming on is number 31 Alex Kacaniklic".